awakening
AT
LOURDES

"The very word 'Lourdes' speaks of healing, love, and consolation. Our Mother, Mary, and her son, Jesus, are so evident there. To savor these tender reflections by another mom, Christy Wilkens, only enhances the power of that word 'Lourdes'!"

Cardinal Timothy Dolan
Archbishop of New York
and conventual chaplain ad honorem of the Order of Malta

"Pilgrimages cost us something, as Christy Wilkens reminds us. But that cost can change us in profound ways. As Wilkens shares the story of her son's miraculous experience at the famed baths, I was equally struck by her refreshing candor as she recounts how her unbelief became an unshakeable "Yes, Lord." Careful, this book may just change you, too."

Kathryn Whitaker
Author *Live Big, Love Bigger*

"If you've ever wondered what happens while on pilgrimage to Lourdes, this is a great place to begin that exploration. Christy Wilkens brilliantly captures the joy, blessing, and true sense of hope her family received while on their faith-filled pilgrimage to find healing for their young son Oscar. Let yourself be drawn in to this powerful account and experience vicariously the beautiful culture and faith Lourdes is known for. I promise that by the final sentence you will be booking your flight."

Mary E. Lenaburg
Author of *Be Brave in the Scared*

"Many people who are sick seek the intercession of Our Lady of Lourdes for healing, but what happens when they don't get their requested miracle? They discover the other miracles along the way. This is the story of the Wilkens family."

Fr. Edward Looney
Author of *A Heart Like Mary's*

"Christy Wilkens's insights go far beyond the beautiful details of experiencing Lourdes. Not only does she show us what receiving a miracle means but she also reveals how God knows far better than we do what our needs are. Readers will join a swarm of believers, along with a few humble doubters, on this journey to Lourdes to experience through Wilkens's eyes and heart what a Lourdes pilgrimage truly does for one's faith and life."

Michelle Buckman
Author, international speaker, and writing workshop instructor

"In vivid and lyrical prose, Christy Wilkens shares with us the most intimate details of a pilgrimage that was both physical and spiritual. From gut-wrenchingly raw moments to periods filled with the kind of peace that can only come from true joy, Wilkens's story carries us away until we are forced to admit to ourselves that, despite our flaws, we are all unconditionally loved by our Creator God."

Amy J. Cattapan
Catholic author, teacher, and member of the
Order of Malta American Association

"In this honest, piercing story of brokenness and blessing, Christy Wilkens is a narrator we come to love and trust. Beyond that, we fall in love with her family—in particular, her son Oscar—as they seek a path toward wholeness. Their challenging, difficult journey is one full of grace, love, and redemption."

Kate Rademacher
Author of *Following the Red Bird*

"You will recognize your own story in these pages. And you will walk away knowing, on a soul level, one of the most essential truths any of us could ever hope to understand: your brokenness is not just something to be endured; it may very well turn out to be your greatest blessing."

From the foreword by **Jennifer Fulwiler**

"In *Awakening at Lourdes*, Christy Wilkens spins a powerful tale of suffering and redemption, describing her journey to Lourdes with her son and husband and the miracles that ensued. Wilkens's writing is luminous—full of heart, raw honesty, and touches of humor and both intensely personal and universal in its insights. Her reflections on the many varieties of healing bring the gift of Lourdes to everyone who reads her words."

Lori Erickson
Author of *Holy Rover* and *Near the Exit*

"In a world where strength and health are so often equated with blessing and merit, Christy Wilkens asks us to question everything we thought we knew of healing. This book gracefully challenges our assumptions about what makes a miracle and extends an invitation to find God, not outside of our present reality but right here in the middle of it."

Shannon K. Evans
Author of *Embracing Weakness*

awakening
AT
LOURDES

HOW AN UNANSWERED PRAYER
HEALED OUR FAMILY AND
Restored Our Faith

CHRISTY WILKENS

AVE MARIA PRESS AVE Notre Dame, Indiana

Founded in 1865, Ave Maria Press is a ministry of the United States Province of Holy Cross.

www.avemariapress.com

Paperback: ISBN-13 978-1-64680-111-4

E-book: ISBN-13 978-1-64680-112-1

Cover image © Terry Harris @Alamy Stock Photo www.alamy.com.

Cover and text design by Katherine Robinson.

Printed and bound in the United States of America.

Library of Congress Cataloging-in-Publication Data
Names: Wilkens, Christy, author.
Title: Awakening at Lourdes : how an unanswered prayer healed our family and restored our faith / Christy Wilkens.
Description: Notre Dame, IN : Ave Maria Press, [2021] | Summary: "In this book, the author recounts her experience bringing her profoundly disabled son to Lourdes, where she and her family found community and healing"-- Provided by publisher.
Identifiers: LCCN 2021020954 (print) | LCCN 2021020955 (ebook) | ISBN 9781646801114 (paperback) | ISBN 9781646801121 (ebook)
Subjects: LCSH: Catholic families--Religious life. | Sanctuaire Notre-Dame de Lourdes (Lourdes, France) | Christian pilgrims and pilgrimages--France--Lourdes. | Parents of chronically ill children--United States--Biography. | Wilkens, Oscar Thomas. | BISAC: RELIGION / Christianity / Catholic | RELIGION / Christian Living / Spiritual Growth
Classification: LCC BX2351 .W55 2021 (print) | LCC BX2351 (ebook) | DDC 232.91/7094478--dc23
LC record available at https://lccn.loc.gov/2021020954
LC ebook record available at https://lccn.loc.gov/2021020955

DEDICATED TO THE 2017 MALADES

OF THE

ORDER OF MALTA AMERICAN ASSOCIATION,

ESPECIALLY THE CHILDREN

CONTENTS

Foreword by Jennifer Fulwiler **xi**

1. Little Earthquakes **1**

2. Together, Alone **9**

3. The Brink **17**

4. We Are in France **25**

5. Malade **31**

6. My Faith Is Not Equal to My Situation **37**

7. On Holding On and Letting Go **43**

8. Prostrate in the Mud **51**

9. Gethsemane **61**

10. Raise You Up **71**

11. The Dark Night of the Soul **79**

12. Water, Fire, and a Cave **85**

13. Lowered through the Roof **93**

14. Outward Signs, Inward Grace **99**

15. Nothing a Bottle of Wine Can't Solve **107**

16. The Beloved **113**

17. Crêpes au Chocolat **121**

18. In the Footsteps of Bernadette **127**

19. Sealed with the Gifts **135**

20. Life Wins **139**

21. Our Lady of Lourdes **149**

22. The Other Brink **157**

23. What I Have Seen and Heard **165**

24. Rise, Take Up Your Mat **173**

25. Chosen, Blessed, Broken, Given **179**

Epilogue **185**

Acknowledgments **191**

Ecce, Fiat, Magnificat: A Discussion Guide on the Healing Power of Surrender and Community **195**

Notes **209**

Foreword

One of the salient aspects of modern Western society is an obsession with health and bodily perfection. You can't drive past a billboard or scroll past an online ad without being bombarded with messages that you are "less than" if you are not young, beautiful, and in peak health. These messages carry dark ideas that are more pernicious and destructive than we realize. Parents feel pressure to terminate pregnancies of babies who might need special care. The sick and the elderly at best feel as if they are burdens to their communities—and at worst are encouraged to consider assisted suicide.

St. John Paul II labeled this troubling cultural landscape a "culture of death." Now more than ever, Christians must combat this worldview by boldly proclaiming a culture of life. We must affirm the beauty of human life in all its states and stages, both when we are in vibrant health and when we are malades. Yet words aren't enough. We need to be witnesses. We need to bring the world around us into personal stories of joy in the midst of suffering, stories of redemption in pain—and that is exactly what Christy Wilkens does in these pages.

In this vividly written book, Christy brings us in to the intimate moments of her family's journey with their son, Oscar. She never holds back about the difficulties of having a child with significant special needs: hurtful comments from others, the strain it puts on a marriage, feeling stressed and embarrassed by public outbursts from a child who is so often misunderstood. She also introduces us to other families who face grueling medical issues and gives us a glimpse of their realities as well. This is not a book that offers glib anecdotes and glosses over real pain; Christy has the courage to tell it like it really is.

Yet she is also unflinching in sharing the good. She dares us not to recoil from the pain she has experienced, but to stick with her as she weaves this tale, so that we're right there with her when she is flooded with profound gratitude and wonder after seeing God move in impossible situations. We wipe our tears and jump for joy along with her when we are reminded over and over again that God often answers prayers very differently than we had hoped, but his plans are always so, so much better than our own.

In some way or another, every single one of us is a malade. Whether you have a child with special needs or not, whether you are in great or poor health, you will recognize your own story in these pages. And you will walk away knowing, on a soul level, one of the most essential truths any of us could ever hope to understand: your brokenness is not just something to be endured; it may very well turn out to be your greatest blessing.

Jennifer Fulwiler

1.

LITTLE EARTHQUAKES

Oscar Thomas Wilkens, our unexpected sixth child, was born on the second Sunday of Advent, a day dedicated to peace amid the dizzying preparations of Christmas. My husband, Todd, had led family prayers asking God (no, begging!) for more peace in our lives every night for years; we rejoiced in the liturgical timing of Oscar's arrival as an answer to that constant prayer. Oscar's birthday was also the feast day of St. Nicholas, the patron saint of children. We baptized Oscar at our Catholic parish in Austin, Texas, on the Feast of the Holy Family.

Oscar may not have been part of our plans, but his birth seemed to be a heavenly response from God. Peace. Children. Holy Family. These cosmic confluences were a confirmation that we were following God's will for our family, even when his will seemed heavy and complicated. (And loud. Our house is really, really loud.)

Oscar's birth changed everything, in the way that these things usually change when a new human makes his acquaintance with the world. We fell in love, the angels danced, and the stars and planets aligned as our family welcomed our beautiful, perfect, matchless boy.

Exactly five months later, our beautiful, perfect, matchless boy began seizing in my arms during the very first hour of a retreat for mothers. While a beatific, smiling nun offered me and my fellow retreatants an impassioned exhortation about the spirituality of motherhood, Oscar offered an entirely different one of his own.

Let me tell you a secret about the spirituality of motherhood: suffering is required. Suffering comes to all of us, parent and child alike, in one form or another. It creeps in during the night or in broad daylight. It catches at your child's breath, or his heart, or her right arm—or his brain. When your life is inextricably entwined with that of another, and a sliver of your inmost being is walking around inside another body, your sufferings are entwined as well. Love is impossible without opening your heart to suffering. Loving well means baring all the nerves of your body and tendrils of your soul wide open.

Suffering can draw us directly into the heart of Christ—not only us, but the people who surround us too. Suffering is not meant to be borne alone. It cries out to be shared, and that cry calls forth love in action, and wherever charity and love exist, God comes to dwell. Bearing suffering well is one of the surest paths to heaven.

This is the story of how I learned to bear mine.

On a clear-skied afternoon in 2016, my mother and I drove out into the remote Texas Hill Country with baby Oscar to spend Mother's Day weekend at a retreat hosted by the Dominican Sisters of Mary, Mother of the Eucharist.

After unpacking, we filed in to the spacious, light-soaked chapel. During Vespers, the evening prayer of the universal Church, Oscar nursed contentedly in my arms and my shoulders relaxed, the weight of my daily cares slipping from them, borne away by the sisters' steady chanting. By the time Sister Joseph Andrew began her opening talk, he had dozed off in my lap, snuggled sideways against my chest, breathing evenly, a trail of milk dribbling from his rosy bow lips. About twenty minutes later, Sister was still speaking about feminine virtue and the spiritual gifts of motherhood, and my pacified mind was beginning to wander, when Oscar awoke with a very sudden, very violent jerk.

I looked down quickly, expecting him to start crying. Instead, his wide, sea-blue eyes gazed up at me with surprise, then wonder, then joy. An instant later, those eyes went vacant, his smile stretched into a grimace, and his arms and legs all stiffened in unison.

His limbs began trembling, spasmodically, forcefully. I clutched him harder to keep him from shaking right off my lap, while I stared in disbelief. For several eternal seconds, I couldn't understand what was happening. Then a single word coalesced in my brain:

Seizure.

I stood and began to awkwardly, frantically climb over several seated women to reach the end of the row, cradling a shaking Oscar tightly against my chest all the while. Without a plan, I thumped backward through the heavy double doors.

Throughout my acrobatics, Oscar kept seizing. He was rigid, shaking, unresponsive, and his face was getting redder and redder. Foamy puddles formed at the corners of his mouth and spilled down his chin. We were miles from the nearest hospital and out of cell-phone range; primitive instinct swamped logic, and I huddled with him in an empty, shady corner, falling back on the muscle memory of motherhood, the familiar motions and words of rocking a fussy baby. They were woefully inadequate to the task at hand, but they were all I had. "It's okay, my love. Mama's here. Shh."

After ninety seconds that stretched into eternity, the shaking slowed. His limbs relaxed. The light came back into Oscar's eyes, locked now on mine. His arms and legs began jerking again, this time in unison, slowly and rhythmically, whole-body hiccups. His gorgeous blue eyes grew unfathomably deep, looking at something above and beyond me. Suddenly, Oscar's face was overcome with a smile not his own. It looked radiant, otherworldly—positively angelic—as his limbs kept hiccupping.

He's saying goodbye, I thought, panic rising in my chest. The world spun and receded. All I could see was my son's face, fixed in a spotlight, smiling that unnatural, peaceful smile. *The next thing that is going to happen is he will stop breathing. He is smiling like that because he knows he is about to die.*

But he didn't die. Instead, the jerking slowed, then subsided. His smile faded, his eyes clouded, and Oscar began to wail.

My mother joined me outside, and we tried to hold a tense, hurried discussion, while Oscar screamed and screamed. One of the nuns came over and asked to help him; I hesitated. Was it irresponsible to say yes, to hand him over to a stranger after such a freakish episode? I laid him in her arms, and she enfolded Oscar in her white robes, swishing back and forth down the crushed gravel path in smooth, rocking motions. The sun was setting just behind the two of them; their bodies pressed together blocked the light. They were framed by the pink and golden glow of the immense Texas sky, cedars and hills falling away below them. Their peaceful silhouette betrayed nothing of the specter that loomed over my son.

Less than three hours after arriving, we packed up and left, bound for the children's hospital. As soon as we explained to the sisters what had happened, the entire retreat—a hundred consecrated nuns and lay women, spiritual mothers and the regular bodily kind—began to pray for Oscar.

These were the first. Many would follow.

Until Oscar's first seizure, if you had asked anyone who knew me, you would have been informed that I was a devout and faithful Catholic. I had reverted to the religion of my childhood in my midtwenties, after ten years of resisting it with all my might. My husband, a convert from agnosticism, embraced his fledgling faith at the same time. The reality that both of us crossed from a life of secularism to a life of Catholicism *together* was a singular grace for our young marriage, during the middle weeks of my first pregnancy.

But a crack in that faith now opened, a weakening that would widen and spread from end to end.

A few months after the incident, on a brazenly bright September day, the kind where the southern sunlight forces you to walk squinting down at the pavement, I sat in the adoration chapel of my home parish. Sunlight filtered through innumerable shards of colored glass, casting rainbow reflections across the marble walls and onto my two fists, balled in my lap as I sat in the solitude of that sacred space. The only sounds were the whoosh of my heartbeat filling my eardrums and the scrape of my ragged breath, in and out like knives.

I had come to the chapel that day for the first time in months. I had come to beg for a reprieve, a do-over. I had asked Jesus, "Please. Please. Can this just be something he will get over? Please, won't you make this all go away and make my son whole again?"

I had not come intending to pray that prayer, or even to pray. My prayers had dried up like the creeks and lakes around us during the long, hot days of that summer, leaving only an occasional fossilized footprint along the dry beds of my spiritual practice. Adoration had been, at other points in my life, a weekly habit of mine, but this visit to the adoration chapel was my first since the Mother's Day retreat—since it had become apparent that Oscar's was not the "good" kind of childhood epilepsy, easily managed, easily outgrown.

Our parish's adoration chapel is small, intimate, and beautiful. Stained glass windows with remarkable, lifelike detailing line the upper half of the two exterior walls. All the chairs and kneelers face the Blessed Sacrament displayed through a transparent opening in a monstrance—an elaborate, jewel-encrusted sunburst perched atop a stand—revealing Christ to those assembled. Catholics believe that Christ is literally present in the Sacrament: not present in a mystical or symbolic way, but fully and completely present—body and blood, soul and divinity—mysteriously clothed under the appearance of bread. The chapel is a place where anyone can go to sit in Jesus' literal presence.

My visit was intended to be a momentary drop-in. I had a few hours to spare and no kids in tow, and it was meant to be a baby step—five minutes, tops, with my Lord and Savior, like the tortured adolescent gracing the family living room just long enough to ask for her allowance and the car keys. Jesus and I were barely on speaking terms.

I began with centering breaths, trying to clear my mind, then followed with a few of the Catholic prayers I knew so well I could say them in my sleep: an Our Father, a Hail Mary, and a Glory Be. I breathed in and out, forming three simple words that anchored my prayers to my breath.

Ecce. "Behold, your child is here before you, Lord, broken and tired." The time between the breaths was for an acceptance of my own smallness.

Fiat. "Let it be done; please help me to accept your will for me today." I inhaled the silent power of God, his grace, his goodness, his almighty power, the reception of God's gifts and his plan.

Magnificat. "My soul magnifies the Lord, the Lord who I know is good and loves me no matter what." I exhaled the word as an offering.

This slow inhale and exhale with the three simple words of prayer had been a practice dear to me for years, since I first read about it in a book, *Consoling the Heart of Jesus* by Fr. Michael Gaitley. The steady exchange of oxygen and carbon dioxide, acceptance and praise, usually worked when nothing else would. Lately, nothing else would.

Before I had gathered more than a dozen of these slow, intentional breaths, the thing I had been hiding in my heart crept out and announced itself unbidden. I whispered the words that reflected the deepest, the truest, the only cry of my heart: "Please, Lord. Please. Heal my son."

Secluded with Jesus for all of ten minutes, I had been admiring the stained glass windows as I meditated. Suddenly, those windows sprang to life.

That might have been a helpful aid to my contemplation if the windows had been of charming biblical scenes: Noah's ark and the rainbow! The nativity, with happy angels and shepherds singing Gloria! But no, the windows in our chapel shone forth pain and anguish, like destroying angels. One showed seven swords piercing the heart of Mary, representing the seven moments when mothering Jesus cost Mary her own excruciating pain. Another depicted the Pietà, the moment when Mary received in her arms the dead, bloody body of her son.

Over and over again, the Pietà, the Pietà.

The visions played themselves wildly before my eyes while I sat rooted to my spot, ensnared so deeply I couldn't even cry. All the pain in the entire world poured into my heart like molten lead, burning me alive from the inside out.

My vision went dark. The roaring pain went dull. I heard interior words, but not my own, as clearly as a tolling bell.

This is your cross, and I am not going to take it away from you. I will be with you, and I will help you, but it is yours to carry.

Sometimes, to this day, I wish I could go back, take my old self by the shoulders, and whisper to her, "See? See here? *He will be with you, and he will help you.*" From the very first seconds, Jesus had shown up. He sent my mother with me that weekend so that I did not face the most terrifying moment of my life alone. He prodded that nun to walk over and comfort my inconsolable child. He blanketed our family in the prayers of community from the precise inflection point when our Before became After.

What I received in those words in the chapel was a deluge, an epic flood to refill the parched creek beds of my soul, but what I thought I received was a curse.

What Jesus was telling me was *I will be with you, and I will help you.*

But I had asked him to heal my son, so what I heard him say was "No."

2.

Together, Alone

Almost one year to the day after Oscar's first seizure at the retreat, I stood before Gate B23 in John F. Kennedy International Airport, near an eight-foot-tall sign bearing a white cross on a red shield. Oscar lay quietly in his stroller next to me. I watched surreptitiously from behind a pillar as two women wearing name tags that matched the banner chatted enthusiastically. When a couple approached the counter, the women greeted them with warm hugs and ushered them to elevator doors that swallowed them away to a hidden fate.

I inhaled all the courage I could glean from the stale air, thick with the bouquet of ripe travelers, trying to bury my shyness and uncertainty. Then I pushed Oscar's stroller toward the desk.

"Hi. I'm Christy Wilkens, and this is Oscar. He's one of the malades."

Malade is a French word meaning "sick." I had first heard it used in this context, referring to sick people, while reading the blog of Catholic author Mary Lenaburg. Mary's daughter, Courtney, had a medical history like Oscar's—a history that had unfolded for the past twelve months like a slow-motion train wreck. Mary wrote poignant, honest reflections about her life raising (and losing) Courtney, including the story of their trip to Lourdes, France, as guests of a group called the Order of Malta.

Oscar, Todd, and I were embarking on the same pilgrimage, hosted annually by the same group. We had nothing left to lose; nothing else so far had worked. The further illumination of Oscar's case had revealed one crevice after another, each harboring a new devastation. Day after day, doctors reassured us that they had a plan. *It's probably this*, they would explain, *so we'll try that.*

Day after day, Oscar stymied their optimistic theories.

At first, I clung tenaciously to the hope that we were just one more medication, one more try, from the solution that would return our story to rights. We chased "normal." Our friends joined us in begging for "complete healing." I loved my son, and I wanted him well and whole. I wanted God to reveal his glory in one particular and precise way: through the total restoration of our child's health. I prayed for this, aloud, in indelible ink, unashamedly.

In secret, doubts were floating in like milkweed seeds, drifting stealthily to the ground, taking invisible root. And by the end of the first summer, the words our medical team used during consults were not "usually" or "probably." They were "tricky" and "complicated."

I chased down more information, second and third opinions. One sympathetic nurse gave us a book called *Seizures and Epilepsy in Childhood: A Guide*, which I scrutinized from cover to cover, with an obsession bordering on pathological. It turned out to be a "so your kid has had a seizure" kind of book, hopeful and reassuring. *Will my child still be able to ride a bike?*

Ride a bike? I worried about whether my child would ever be able to feed himself solid food, ideally without aspirating it into his lungs. I whipped the book angrily across the room, watching it somersault through the air.

Oscar's neurologist was one we had met the morning after Oscar's first seizure, during an overnight EEG in the hospital; she had discharged us with an all-clear and the words, "I hope we never see each other again!" (We saw each other quite regularly now.) After recounting the litany of unknowns and unclear test results, I told her about the book.

I spat out venomously, "That book was not written for us. We are off the map."

She instantly agreed. We inhabited a new world, one featuring pitiless, honest answers as daily bread.

My prayers grew thick in my mouth, hard to swallow, harder to spit out. I continued to ask our friends and family for their prayers, while my own practice shrank and shrank. The Rosaries stopped. The evening family prayer grew inconsistent, then sporadic, then it stopped too. All the Bibles gathered a thick layer of dust.

Really, I had no idea what to pray for. The only thing I wanted had been denied me. *This is your cross, and I am not going to take it away from you.* At that blow, my son and I were each paralyzed in our own way. God told me, without mincing words, that complete healing was possible, but not for Oscar. This body was the body he would have. There would be no glorious, miraculous restoration.

I knew that we were supposed to offer up suffering, that by uniting it to the cross it could be transformed into a kind of selfless, life-giving joy. Countless saints have written countless pages about this. In many ways, *the defining characteristic* of a Christian is to bear trials with patience, hope, and joy. The ideal attitude is perfect trust: if God has allowed suffering, then his reasons, however inscrutable, must be good.

And yet now that I was squarely—and apparently irretrievably—in the middle of such suffering, I found I was incapable of accepting it. If I couldn't understand how to hope, I couldn't let myself feel it or live it. I resigned myself, instead, to living the rest of my life with the tremendous betrayal I had felt ever since that day in the adoration chapel. That day had been the last time I heard from God for a long time. Effortlessly, instantly, I built a wall around my heart. *Okay, you're not going to heal my son? Fine. Then I will handle this. I will just get on without you.*

And so, he let me.

Why, then, was I standing in the middle of this airport with my husband, preparing to fly our son halfway around the world? I clung to God as a life preserver, a purely mechanical means to keep from drowning under the weight of my despair. Without hope, without love, I kept God around to use him, test him. Having exhausted the medical possibilities for healing our son, I wanted to trick the Creator of the Universe into doing it on command, like a two-bit magician.

Back at the gate counter in JFK airport, a tanned, polished woman arrived, wearing a red cardigan that set off her perfectly coiffed dark bob. The two ladies already there waved her in our direction. She walked up and said, "Hi, Christy, I'm Kim Gillespie." She pulled me into a hug without a pause, her compact energy like a coiled spring. Every movement of hers exuded confidence, and I relaxed almost against my will, in grateful recognition of the arrival of an alpha female.

Kim was Oscar's "pod host," a term at which I had nodded blankly the week before, when she introduced herself during one of a dizzying barrage of phone calls explaining last-minute details. Now she explained more fully: "Our job is to take care of you this week. We'll have some other little duties here and there, but our most important job is Oscar."

"Wait, you mean *just* Oscar? I thought all the volunteers took care of everybody."

She shook her head and fixed me with her gaze, unwavering and direct. "No. Each pod is a single team assigned to a specific malade— and *only* that malade."

I blinked. Somehow, I had assumed that the people in our pod would come and go throughout the week. But the opposite was true: *Oscar* was the pod's responsibility. They might have other small duties, but their job was to serve him, first and foremost. She explained that Oscar's pod had three other members too. We would sit together on the plane, eat meals together, room near each other, and walk in procession as one group.

Todd, who had been wading through the pilgrimage registration on our behalf, finally appeared at my side. As I introduced him, another member of our pod, Carole Less, arrived. Kim was friendly in an assertive, East Coast kind of way, but Carole was a social butterfly, almost visibly sparkling, delighted to get her hands on Oscar. After two minutes of cursory introductions, she grabbed Oscar's stroller and said, "Why don't you two go get a drink? I'll take him for a walk around the terminal." Without waiting for a response, she wheeled around and disappeared into the crowded international airport with our medically fragile son.

Todd and I gaped at each other.

Kim chuckled at our expressions and commanded, "You're not going to see them for a while. You might as well do what she said and get that drink."

Just like that, we found ourselves alone together—an exceedingly rare and precious opportunity for parents of six. We clasped hands and meandered down the terminal, shaking our heads in a daze and trying to decide where to go, settling on a splurge in the Delta Lounge.

While I did my best to luxuriate in every bite and sip, as the minutes ticked by, I couldn't keep my mind focused on our mini-date. I kept glancing at the door and the clock on my phone.

Todd read my heart in my eyes. "He's going to be fine. We came here to let people help us take care of him."

"I know. But—she just took him. She doesn't know anything about him, and he doesn't know her. Do we even have her phone number?"

"We have Kim's. Don't worry. But if you really want to go back, we can."

"No, let's stay. Let's finish lunch." A long pause, during which I took another half-hearted sip of my wine. "And then we'll go back and check in as soon as we're done."

By the time we took our last bites, my mind was awhirl, and Todd could tell I was barely listening to what he was saying. We grabbed our bags and began the walk back to the gate, my stride getting longer and faster with each step.

He grabbed my hand and squeezed. "He's fine. He's going to be fine."

"I know." I quickened my pace anyway, straining to see any glimpse of the vivid blue stroller.

About fifty yards down the terminal, I finally spotted them, and the breath that had been caught in my throat escaped with a sigh. My pilgrim act of surrender and trust apparently needed some work.

We caught up with Carole and Kim, who introduced us to Ryan Young, another team member. Ryan was a tall, solidly built man with a ready smile and piercing laugh, which he immediately put to good use when we needled him about being assigned to the smallest, lightest malade on the pilgrimage.

The wine had wound its way through my bloodstream, and I was beginning to feel relaxed with this new little pod-family materializing around us. But where were Oscar's fellow malades? Who else had chosen to uproot themselves from their daily lives and throw themselves on the mercy of Jesus, chasing miracles? We made our way downstairs to the Order's designated waiting area, the epitome of airport bleakness: cement floor, cheerless walls, unyielding molded plastic seats. Despite the stark atmosphere, it was alive with nervous anticipation and stuffed absolutely to bursting with people standing, sitting, in wheelchairs, on stretchers.

Someone tried to call the room to attention so that a priest could give a short reflection. Even though the room fell nearly silent, it was so packed with bodies that the priest's voice was absorbed into nothingness. The silent and prayerful attention birthed a moment of communion—timelessness took possession of the entire room like an embrace—then we pilgrims were released back into a stuffy terminal with a rush of noise.

I felt an immediate and ferocious affection for everyone in the room—hundreds of fellow Catholics I had never seen before. Then I felt an equally ferocious desire to shake it off, to remain apart. I had trained myself, for twelve brutal months, to guard my heart from friends and from Jesus—even from Todd. Preserving control and distance was the only way I knew to keep myself from being overwhelmed by disappointment as Oscar's situation turned from tricky to bad, from bad to worse, from worse to unendurable.

When Christ walked the earth, though, he founded a community. He built a Church full of people, many of them flawed and ridiculous, and then left *them* with instructions about how to worship, live, love, and keep building. Over the decade since my return to the faith, Christ tried to remind me of this often during conversation in prayer.

"You are part of the Body of Christ," he insisted, over and over. "One member alone cannot be the whole Body."

"Yes, Lord, I know," I would reply. "I'm part of the Body. But I'm just going to do my part *over here*. You know, *alone*. I'm just going to kind of sit on the edge, if you don't mind." My life had been always lived at the edge: the edge of the crowd at parties, the edge of commitment to plans in case I wanted to change my mind.

Jesus called, softly and tenderly, in many ways, through many voices, and I refused to take the hint. After Oscar's seizures began, well-meaning people trooped in with the best reassurance they knew how to offer, holding placards and banners and bullhorns proclaiming that tiresome adage:

God never gives you more than you can handle!

Reader, I assure you, he most certainly does. And he usually does it because it's the most expedient way to communicate one insurmountable truth:

None of us is meant to endure the trials of this life alone.

3.

THE BRINK

As we neared our boarding time, the entire pilgrimage group—all four hundred of us—began to congregate around the departure gate. The noise of so many people in close quarters was a solid wall of sound. The temperature rose as the bodies packed in together.

A movement from the stroller caught my eye. Oscar was rolling his head from side to side, like a terrible Stevie Wonder impression. As he continued the rhythmic, robotic motion, his eyes rolled back in his head. His jaw began chewing even though his mouth was empty.

He was having a seizure. It was his first seizure in five months. We had battled like knights errant for control over these seizures, discarding one medication after another with increasing desperation and panic, until a pair of delicately calibrated therapies did the trick. Today of all days, the seizure beast reawakened, slouching toward our son to reclaim his brain.

I tugged Todd down to look at him with me. "What is this? He's never had one like this before."

We began our standard protocol for weird seizure-like movements: tap on his nose and call his name. "Oscar? Oscar! Hey, buddy, look at me." He did not blink. He did not cease his rolling and chewing. His eyes stayed glued to the tops of his eye sockets, almost nothing showing but whites. He was clearly seizing, but we were in unfamiliar territory here. This was nothing like his old patterns—a completely, terrifyingly new seizure type.

Now we had the attention of Carole and Kim too. I had been counting silently in my head, instinctually, and realized we were already closing in on the one-minute mark. The seizure wasn't stopping. It wasn't even slowing; it intensified.

Todd continued talking to Oscar. "Hey, Oscar, look at Papa. Wake up, Oscar. Come on, buddy, wake up." I rummaged through our diaper bag until my fingers closed around a six-inch-long plunger. Oscar's rescue medication, diazepam. Never in a year of seizures had we needed it. More than once, we had left the house without it. The doctor had prescribed it as a remote precaution. The medication was a strong sedative, similar to Valium. It should calm the seizure within a minute.

But it carried this ominous instruction: once administered, we had to call an ambulance immediately and stay on the line with the dispatch. Not only did the medication slow down brain function to suppress the seizure, but it slowed down every other autonomic function controlled by the brain. Breathing. Heartbeat.

In other words, the rescue medication guaranteed an ambulance ride to the emergency room, instead of a plane ride to Lourdes.

I turned back to Oscar while clutching the diazepam in one hand, rubbing his leg with the other. A voice over my shoulder asked, "How long has the seizure been going on?"

"Maybe a minute and a half?" I turned my head, realizing the question hadn't come from anyone on our pod. A stout, dark-haired woman behind me introduced herself, cell phone pressed to her ear. "I'm Selma, one of the nurses," she said to me, peering at Oscar carefully and then turning away.

"Oh, thank God. Could you please call the neurologist? I need to know whether to give his rescue med." *Please, God, please no.*

Carole patted my elbow gently. "She's already on the phone with him."

The seconds dragged on torturously until the neurologist pushed his way through the crowd, following Selma's precise directions. He shook my hand firmly. "I'm Dr. Kearney." Without any other niceties, he studied Oscar, then nodded. "It's a focal seizure, but it's not generalizing. I'm not too worried. He's going to be okay; I think we can wait it out. How long has it been?"

"Over two minutes, maybe three," I answered. "He's never had a seizure like this before. I wasn't sure whether we needed to give him diazepam."

He shook his head and a wave of relief swept over me, so strong it carried nausea in its wake. "No, this won't cause any permanent damage. We shouldn't need it."

Todd jumped in. "It seems as if the lights and noise are bothering him. He's crazy overstimulated. He's overtired, too, which is a trigger for him." Each time he waved his hand above Oscar, Oscar's chewing slowed almost imperceptibly. He reached over and pulled the stroller shade down.

As soon as the edge of the shade broke the line of Oscar's inhumanly upturned gaze, the intensity of his seizure lessened. His head and jaw slowed, and his eyes bounced up and down instead of staying rolled back. The small crowd around the stroller released a long-held breath, almost in unison.

Todd asked, "It's almost time for his nighttime meds, and some of those are for sleep. Do you think we should give them a little early, to knock out the rest of the seizure?"

The doctor nodded gravely, still watching Oscar closely. "That's a great idea."

I was already rummaging through the medicine bag, setting tiny plastic cups down on the grimy floor, dumping meds into the pill crusher, twisting with practiced expertise. No motion wasted; no seconds wasted. "No, let me hold them." Kim nudged me aside and gathered the cups, holding them as I emptied powders, squirted water, stirred and scraped and filled syringes.

Everyone watched with a combination of horror and awe. "You are incredibly fast at this."

I made our standard joke: "Yes, I'm running my own compounding pharmacy." Not a joke, really. I could mix these meds in my sleep, and never had I been so grateful for those long months of practice. Less than a minute after I started, his nightly cocktail of five medications was ready to go.

By this point, Oscar had calmed enough that he could swallow his medicine, though his eyes were still unfocused and his movements jerky. After the dose, Todd carried him on his shoulder, rocking and bouncing with his own highly practiced rhythm. It took almost no time until Oscar's eyes sagged closed and his body went limp, his breathing steady and deep. Todd gently laid him back in the stroller.

The medical team had saved our pilgrimage from the cliff, then dispersed almost without a word.

My adrenaline rush had subsided, and my entire body shook. Even though I knew how lucky we were to have dodged this bullet, it seemed an indescribable foolishness to take this child across an ocean.

What have I gotten us into?

One of the main spiritual exercises of the pilgrimage was to abandon worry: to trust that God would take care of us, through the hands of these incredibly generous people, even if we didn't know what was going to happen. Hadn't he just shown us exactly that? Hadn't he used these people as instruments to head off a disaster, saving us for an airplane instead of an ambulance?

If we had been traveling alone, I would have used that rescue medication.

But I hadn't. And I noticed: Oscar had received, in this dirty, overcrowded terminal, better care than he usually received in the hospital. A full-fledged neurologist had been at his side in less than two minutes. The neurologist had observed his seizure in real time and made a treatment call based on the evidence of his own eyes, not video footage or our after-the-fact reports. I exhaled thanksgiving for the team that God had assembled. *Fiat.* Let it be done.

I closed my eyes and reached a decision. *Okay, God. I can focus on the scariness and uncertainty, or I can focus on the people you sent to help us. I'm choosing surrender. I'm choosing thanksgiving. Please help me to sustain that choice, because if we weren't already thousands of miles from home, I would pack it in and call it a day.*

In a quiet, unused gate nearby, I cradled Oscar while Carole talked to me continuously for the next hour, as the line of boarding pilgrims shrank and my adrenaline ebbed. I was too weary to do anything but listen; she sensed this intuitively and filled the space between my ears with gentle stories, as if soothing a small child at bedtime. She told me about her interior design business as the passengers in wheelchairs were rolled on. She recounted how her daughter's family had moved in with her as the Order's Knights and Dames shuffled slowly forward. I listened with gratitude, mute and spent, to the one-sided conversation she steered so easily. When the line was down to only a few pilgrims, we strode together down the jet bridge.

I lifted Oscar onto my shoulder, and his head bobbed up and down sleepily. He opened his eyes but snuggled deeper into my neck. As we twisted down the aisle, dodging overhead and underfoot luggage, hands and arms reached out to my son. Faces lit to see a baby in their midst. He nestled contentedly in my arms, spreading that contentment like a lantern glow from one end of the plane to the other.

I busied myself with stowing things in pockets, as Todd buckled Oscar into his car seat, then claimed the center seat for himself, all six feet one inch of his lean body and overgenerous heart. After a welcoming peck on my cheek, Todd nodded to the man sitting directly in front of me. "Hey, that guy wanted to say hi to you."

The man turned around and extended a thickly muscled hand. In heavily accented English, he introduced himself. "Hello! I am Vito." His eyes, framed by heavy, square black spectacles, winked with delight. I liked him instantly, not least because he was an Italian citizen from the same region as my great-grandparents. As we chatted, he rummaged through his satchel and handed me a holy card, his tone shifting to a quiet seriousness. "It's Padre Pio. I have a great devotion to him. Such a holy man, but so simple. Pray, hope, and don't worry, you know that, right?"

"Right, of course." I nodded.

"Todd has been telling me about your son. I know you have been through a lot, but it is good that you are here. I want you to have this. And don't worry."

My eyes filled with tears in an instant. In a flash of fury at myself, I blinked them back and fought for control. I hated that this man I had just met was able to read my soul and reach immediately for the sore spot. Was I that transparent? I am an easy crier, but I had been on the plane for all of five minutes. "Thank you so much, Vito. This means a lot." I struggled to stay composed, chalking up my tears to the potent combination of exhaustion, anticipation, and stress over Oscar's seizure moments before.

Todd, who had been leaning over, smiling, while we chatted, put his arm around my shoulder and thanked Vito with considerably more finesse. We took our seats and began to buckle, although my hands shook visibly and fumbled with the latch. I still held the holy card, and Todd reached over to cradle my unsteady hands in his consoling ones. I concentrated all my effort on projecting poise, but my trembling betrayed me.

"You okay?" he asked.

The tears and self-recrimination both swelled again. I swallowed the lump in my throat and nodded. "Yeah." *No.* What did "okay" even mean anymore? The bar for "okay" seemed permanently set at the ludicrously low standard of "I am not crying right this second."

The plane began taxiing. I thrilled with the familiar excitement, the noise of the jets coupled with the delicious expectancy of knowing you're going somewhere. But then the PTSD I had managed to hold at bay during and after the seizure in the terminal came roaring in. We were now completely trapped in a metal canister for the next seven hours. Any medical emergencies would have to be dealt with here. I gripped my thighs and uttered silent, desperate prayers.

I lived my daily life according to a very formulaic control. We went to a strictly limited set of places, within an easy drive of doctors and hospitals, always in cell phone range. Our lives were now outside my carefully curated sphere of safety. As it turned out, the only thing that couldn't hold together outside that sphere was . . . me.

Oscar slumbered peacefully in his seat, oblivious to the churning in my mind, but Todd was alert to my tension. He reached again for my hands, leaning forward to catch my eyes, which were boring a hole into the seat-back pocket in front of me. "Everything is going to be okay. He's okay."

I nodded. My knuckles whitened.

"Nothing bad is going to happen. We are surrounded by doctors and nurses. And priests! This is the safest place he could possibly be right now on the entire planet."

I loosened my grip, steadied my breath again, and managed another nod. A wayward tear finally loosed itself from captivity and rolled down my cheek.

"You have to surrender. We are on pilgrimage. Surrender, and let things happen the way they're going to happen. That seizure was not an accident. God was showing us that he will take care of us. You have to trust him."

I closed my eyes at that, and Todd, knowing me all too well, stopped talking. He kept hold of my hands, though, and I kept breathing slowly, every breath a prayer for which I had only borrowed words. *Ecce. Fiat. Magnificat.* But mostly, *Ecce, ecce. Here I am, Lord. I don't know exactly why I'm here, but behold, here I am.* By the time we hit the runway, I was ready. I turned to face my husband with a genuine, albeit tentative, smile.

"We're taking our son to Lourdes."

He kissed me again, full on the lips, and settled his head back against his seat. "Yes. We are. Thanks be to God."

4.

WE ARE IN FRANCE

We disembarked into a long hallway lined with windows, showcasing a fairytale landscape.

The planes on the tarmac were dwarfed by the majestic peaks of the snow-capped Pyrenees and a blindingly sunny sky. I knew Lourdes was in the foothills of the mountain range, but I had never expected mere foothills to be so breathtaking. They were craggy, gray, and ancient, both remote and inviting at the same time. Try as I might, my camera refused to record the grandeur—the mountains receded into mist on the screen. When I lowered the lens, they reigned over the entire skyline once again. I abandoned the effort of trying to shoot landscape photography with my smartphone in one hand and twenty-five precariously balanced pounds of limp baby in the other.

Moments later, Todd appeared in line a bit behind us, zigzagging the stroller between passengers and pushing his way forward. I gratefully set Oscar into the stroller. Oscar immediately settled back to his pattern of gazing around contentedly at nothing in particular, sucking his pacifier, and rubbing the hair on the top of his head with one hand. We passed through customs, collected our bureaucratic rubber stamp, and stepped into the springtime mountain air of a glorious morning in Lourdes.

Lourdes is the site where the Virgin Mary appeared to a teenaged French peasant, Bernadette Soubirous, in 1858. Bernadette's family had once been prosperous millers in the town, but they had fallen into poverty so crushing that they were forced to move into a single room. The room had formerly housed a prison, until it had been deemed unfit for convicts and given over to pigs. The dampness exacerbated Bernadette's asthma and threatened her frail constitution. She was so sickly that, despite their poverty, Madame Soubirous always made sure that Bernadette alone, of all her children, had socks to wear.

Not a particularly bright child to begin with, Bernadette's learning stagnated when sickliness led to repeated school absences. She was small for her age and weak. She had great difficulty learning her catechism.

She was, in effect, an unlikely heroine.

One bleak day in February, Bernadette set out with her sister and a friend to gather firewood at Massabielle, a filthy cave in the forest outside of town that was used as a garbage heap by locals. The other two girls crossed the river, but as Bernadette sat to remove her stockings, a sudden noise of wind caught her attention. When she glanced up at a niche in the cave wall, she saw what she later described as a beautiful young girl dressed in white with a blue sash, holding a rosary, with yellow roses at her feet. Bernadette knelt, took her rosary from her pocket, and began to pray.

Bernadette's story was met with disbelief and skepticism, even derision. Her parents beat her, when they first learned what had happened, and forbade her to return to the grotto.

Throughout February, Bernadette continued to visit the site and see the apparition. Curiosity-seekers, and then true believers, began to come with her. On February 25, the vision instructed Bernadette to "drink at the fountain and wash." When Bernadette turned toward the nearby Gave River, the apparition directed her instead to look under the rocks. A small muddy patch was revealed, and Bernadette dutifully clawed at the ground, trying to drink the turbid water she found, to the disgust of the onlookers.

By the next day, a clear spring was flowing where Bernadette had dug. In March, during another apparition, a local woman who had permanently injured her right hand bathed in the water of the spring, and her hand was instantly healed. Lourdes recorded that event as its first of seventy miraculous physical healings that have been verified since 1858 (and countless more unverified).

Bernadette's own infirmities were never healed by the miraculous waters. She died of tuberculosis in her thirties, in the obscurity of a local convent. But today Lourdes welcomes more than six million visitors per year to the shrine erected on the site where she once knelt to recite her Rosary with *uo petito damizelo*, a small young lady.

On the bus ride to the hotel, Oscar rested on my lap, and I leaned my head against the window, drained but exhilarated. Todd sat next to us, his arm looped through my elbow, fingers entwined with mine. *We are in France*, my thoughts kept repeating in an empty, ridiculous loop. I thought it so many times it became meaningless. *We are in France. We are elephants. We are made of green cheese. We are in France.*

The village roads were the very definition of charming, lined with antique stone-and-stucco houses beside weathered barns, every window trimmed with a lace curtain and a box full of neatly tended flowers. We wound through the small town, admiring the shops, the narrow roads twisting between tidy brick buildings set closer and closer together the deeper we traveled into the heart of Lourdes. Streets just wide enough to be one-lane roads in America instead held cars zipping both directions, with brave (or foolhardy) pedestrians walking along the edge. I cringed at each narrowly missed collision.

Street after street was lined with hotel after hotel: Grand Hotel Moderne. St Louis. Arcade. And finally, Hotel Méditerranée and Hotel

Alba, homes of the Order of Malta American Association's pilgrimage for the week.

Our room wasn't ready, so we entered the dining room. The noon-day light pouring in through the high windows had a harsh quality, a glare that made my head ache. In a single moment, the wave of fatigue I had been holding at bay for hours (days? months?) crashed over me. When I tilted my head and shifted my weight, it cleared a little, and I seized the opportunity to walk to a table without wobbling, barely reaching my chair before my knees gave way.

As Todd walked behind me, pushing Oscar, he noticed I was sagging. He nestled his arm around my waist and leaned in to plant a kiss near my ear, whispering, "Are you okay?"

"I'll be fine. I think I just need to eat something."

We seated ourselves at the table, and courses appeared almost immediately. The first was a salad of beautiful, plump lettuces and sliced tomato, with a light, shaved cheese. Grabbing the tongs, I began to pile my plate, but Carole reached over and placed her hand on mine. "The dressing is all on the bottom. You need to toss it first." I stared back at her, mute and uncomprehending, until she freed the tongs from my grasp, tossed the leaves herself, and passed it back. My concentration barely sufficed to control the tongs and land a small helping on my plate.

Everything in the room seemed too bright now. The noise was too bright. The smiles on people's faces were too bright. I began to wonder if I was having a stroke, then decided that if I could wonder that, I probably wasn't. I quietly ate a few bites of salad, willing my jaw to move up and down, coaxing my throat to constrict and swallow. But the next course, thin slices of pork in a rustic brown gravy, arrived well before I finished.

I closed my eyes for a moment. The table had gone quiet and everyone was watching me closely. Kim asked gently, "Do you need to go lie down?"

Fighting against every anxious instinct sounding alarms about the imminent and complete failure of my pilgrimage, and also not sure I could still speak English, I sighed. "Yes, I do."

In one fluid, decisive motion, Kim pushed back her chair. "Come on. You can lie down in my room." As I stood to follow her, the entire floor tilted sideways, tables waving up and down in my vision.

The carpet in our hallway was striped, and I followed the stripes diligently so as not to walk into a wall. I barely managed to say, "Thank you," before my head hit the pillow and I passed out cold on one of the twin beds.

I opened my eyes and panicked. My mind was refreshed and clear. I must have slept for hours, missed the entire first day of the pilgrimage, and screwed up my body's internal clock for the duration of the trip. I checked the clock.

Forty-seven minutes had passed.

Okay, then. Slight overreaction.

From the window, I took in the view. Flat-fronted hotels with self-effacing marquees, effortlessly conveying that shabby-chic look you can buy brand new in America, lined the promenade across the gray, swift-running river. A soft breeze rustled the leaves of the trees, which stood in proud, tidy rows along the sidewalks. The enormous foothills of the Pyrenees lorded over everything.

I inhaled deeply, shut the window, and stepped out of the room, back into the hallway, not sure what to do next. I wandered outside and found Todd and Oscar sitting with another pilgrim, Hugh, whose wife (another malade) had turned in for a nap as well. The two abandoned husbands had decided to take afternoon coffee on the patio with one of the Knights on Hugh's team, a member of the Order of Malta.

"The Sovereign Military Hospitaller Order of St. John of Jerusalem of Rhodes and of Malta"—it sounded like a secret society. When I first researched their origins, the medieval-looking black capes with flashes of red satin only confirmed this impression. Who were these people?

The Order of Malta dates to the time of the crusades and recently celebrated its nine hundredth anniversary. Founded in Jerusalem, it was originally an order of lay (nonordained) Knights sworn to defend the faith and care for sick pilgrims visiting the Holy Land. Its mission today, upheld by volunteers, lay members, and ordained clergy, is still to defend the faith and to care for the poor and sick. The Order runs medical, social, and humanitarian programs all over the world. But the Order also enjoys a unique and privileged diplomatic position: it issues its own currency and passports and holds permanent observer status at the United Nations.

The more I learned, the more obsessed I became. The Order of Malta organizes a worldwide pilgrimage to Lourdes every year and invites sick people as guests. (*Guests!*) There are three associations in the United States alone, and each invites about fifty malades annually, attended by about 350 volunteers, including an extensive medical team. My first impression defined the pilgrimage as some sick-person lottery. *Congratulations, you've won an all-expenses-paid trip to France to line up for your miraculous healing! YOU get a pilgrimage, and YOU get a pilgrimage—EVERYBODY gets a pilgrimage!*

I might have been missing the point, but then again, I *did* like France.

Todd stood to greet me and introduced everyone; then we headed up to settle into our room, where our luggage had appeared. I tried to relax, depositing Oscar in the crib for a good roll-around while I unpacked our suitcases.

Todd said casually, "I had a really great conversation with Hugh and that Knight this afternoon."

I was far too distracted and fidgety to hear the subtext—that he wanted to talk about it with me. Instead, I arranged Oscar's bedding, picked out the toys for his stroller, mixed up a new batch of formula, and took a shower. I flitted around the room with nervous anticipation.

As he had so often over the years of our marriage, Todd watched me with patient bemusement while I utterly failed to listen to him and did my own thing.

5.

MALADE

Downstairs on the plaza, the Order's American Association was assembling for its first procession of the pilgrimage. Kim explained that pilgrims always march with their team color; ours was white. Along the promenade, stretching across two city blocks, there stood a line of members of the Order who were uniformed in black, red, and white, grouped behind seven different-colored flags that indicated the teams, and interspersed with a line of blue, three-wheeled carts. The cart, called a *voiture*, is the primary mode of transportation for malades in Lourdes. In every procession, malades ride in the voitures, and pedestrians and cars alike make way. Each voiture is steered by members of the Order called charioteers.

Voitures are portable thrones, a sign of the reverence and care lavished on the malades. Even malades who are well enough to walk ride in the voitures, sometimes despite their personal discomfort with the idea. Sitting in a voiture requires a surrender of pride and agency, the first of many tiny surrenders, each one a step toward vulnerability: allowing oneself to be cared for, in a very tender, physical, and even intimate way, by nearly perfect strangers.

I took a seat in our voiture with Oscar nestled on my lap, enveloped by a bright-red fleece blanket with a white, eight-pointed Malta cross on the hem. It was the same cross that had been emblazoned on the banner at airport check-in, so ostentatiously foreign there, but commonplace here in Lourdes.

Gradually our team filtered in, and moments before the procession began our team leader, another brisk New Englander, bustled up and introduced us to a new member: "This is Amy Cattapan. She'll be joining your pod. Amy, this is Oscar!" Then she turned on her heel, on to the next task.

As our procession began, I questioned the wisdom of sitting in this voiture with Oscar. It was our first procession, with a first-time charioteer (Ryan), who was on his first pilgrimage to Lourdes himself. On the straightaways we did fine, save for a few hard stops when the queue backed up. But at every curve, I clutched the side rail and tensed—we swung wide into traffic, we grazed a lamppost, we bashed the knee of someone in a sidewalk cafe. Eventually Kim, in a huff, decided Ryan wasn't doing his job properly. She got behind the voiture and began to push, helping to steer the safest course.

At every street, we caught glimpses of other malades, in other voitures, from other countries. The uniforms of the Order of Malta bear the name of their association, and I began keeping a tally in my head: Belgium, England, France, Netherlands, Bohemia. It was a veritable United Nations of sick people.

Todd and I laughed, calling out all the countries we saw, but suddenly I sobered. The realization slapped me in the face: in every voiture, everywhere we looked, someone was suffering. That someone might be enduring the worst suffering of her life.

I knew I was certainly in the middle of mine.

I was overwhelmed, exhausted anew at the unimaginable scale of human suffering. A glimmer of understanding arose of what it meant to say that Jesus bore the suffering of the entire world on his shoulders on the cross. *This suffering* was what he bore, the suffering of *these* people, and I was only extrapolating from one street corner in a backwater French village. Granted, this particular village was a magnet for sufferers, but in an area of a few acres sat thousands, each carrying a deep brokenness, carting it alongside them in squeaky blue carriages through the crooked streets.

As I looked at each malade, I wondered, *What brought you here?* I knew it must be a terrible thing indeed.

But when I looked again, each of those people was peaceful, even smiling. There was joy in the village, a defiant joy rising from among literal cartloads of pain.

I felt a solidarity in that joy. Our time with Oscar at home had been so isolating and disorienting; few of our friends could relate to the minutiae of our daily experience. Here was our secret club. Here were other people who knew the pharmacy staff by first name. Others whose speed dial included an after-hour triage nurse. Others who knew how to receive bad news stoically, and only fall apart later behind the locked bathroom door with the shower running. Others who had refused to give up and who followed their hearts to the foot of the Blessed Mother, begging for her aid.

We were all here, uniting our suffering. The solidarity in that makeshift, fleeting community was an inexplicable comfort.

Because I was slightly below the heads of everyone else in our procession, people had to go out of their way to speak to me. Sometimes they did, but often the conversation carried on above my head. I appreciated the opportunity to lean back, with my boy's heavy weight solid against my sternum, feeling present in our connected bodies. Boxy European cars rolled past, and tourist wares erupted onto the sidewalks: postcards of every conceivable image of the shrine, empty Mary-shaped plastic bottles to fill with Lourdes's healing water, purses and scarves with the image of Our Lady printed on the side. Hundreds of dangling rosaries evoked memories of rainbow beads dangling in the decidedly less wholesome setting of a Mardi Gras parade. The kitsch factor was colossal, and our colorful parade suddenly seemed, in the context of brazen commercialism, a little ridiculous.

Strutting sick people through the streets of France like celebrities? Whose crazy idea was that?

The Blessed Mother's idea. One of the things she said during the apparitions was that she wanted people to come to Lourdes in procession. The tradition of the voitures was in direct response to that request. Each time an association of the Order of Malta brings malades anywhere "official" in Lourdes, they process. I quieted my inner critic and allowed myself to experience the swaying, bumping, erratic movement of the ride as a prayer in itself, an analogue to the erratic movements of my heart.

Before long, we wound our way across a wider paved road and through a wide gate, one of two main entrances to the sanctuary. The Sanctuary of Our Lady of Lourdes, also known as the Domain, is a massive open area preserved near the city center. Set on acreage surrounding the original spring, the Domain is comprised of the Grotto itself, multiple churches and major basilicas, modern fountains dispensing Lourdes water on demand, the pilgrim baths, a working hospital, a graceful prairie, the offices of the Lourdes Medical Bureau, and the wide gathering plaza we were about to enter. A tall pillar graced each side of the gate we approached, the one on the left bearing a statue of St. Joseph, snuggling the Christ child on his hip. As we passed through St. Joseph's Gate under his watchful gaze and entered the Domain, the tawdry shops and noisy cafes faded out of sight and mind, and a hush fell over the earth.

I had known about Lourdes for most of my life. During my twenties, my grandmother's church choir was planning a European tour, and she begged me to sing with her and join them abroad. "Come down for a rehearsal and meet my director. He will love you. I know you can sing it, *mija*. There won't be any problem."

As always, she was right. She approached so many things in her life with cheerful, almost blind assurance. I didn't recognize it then for what it was: faith in God's will. "All shall be well, and all shall be well, and all manner of thing shall be well," as St. Julian of Norwich and my *abuelita* would say.

I had been raised a cradle Catholic, Mexican on one side and Italian on the other. Once during those tender years, my wisecracking grandfather used a colorful expression in my presence. I gasped in horror, "Grandpa!" He growled, "What are you gonna be, a nun?" When I was a child, my faith and morality were simple and untested.

We went to Mass on Sundays, we went to religion class on Wednesdays, and we prayed grace before dinner.

Like many Gen-Xers, though, my faith hit the skids when I entered high school. Few of my friends practiced faith of any kind, and we rebellious teenagers openly mocked authority in any shape and form. When the time came for my confirmation, I told my parents I wasn't ready, and God bless them, they let me choose for myself.

My grandmother prayed for my return to the faith of my ancestors every single day of the ten years that I spent away from it, and she was more excited than anyone when Todd and I were confirmed together, and our marriage convalidated by the Church, two years after our markedly heathen wedding. Her last trip on earth, two weeks before she died, was to witness the baptism of our third child, who was wearing the gown Grandma had painstakingly embroidered for my own baptism.

She was fierce and tender, charitable and intelligent, witty and kind. But most of all, she was pious and relentless. Whenever we parted after a visit, even during my wandering, faithless years, she would ask me to lean down so she could trace the Sign of the Cross on my forehead and say, "May God's blessing go with you and keep you safe. Amen." Then she would beam at me with a satisfied smile, pointedly ignoring my bemused detachment.

But despite Grandma's prodigious efforts, I wasn't Catholic at the time of the choir tour. Todd (my then-boyfriend) and I decided to make the concerts part of a longer European vacation. We had a lot of ground to cover, so we chose to forego the stops that seemed too overtly religious for our taste. Singing hymns at Catholic pilgrimage sites with my Catholic grandmother and her Catholic choir was a bridge too far for my youthful hubris. We said yes to the Eiffel Tower and no to the grotto of Lourdes.

I think, now, that God was saving Lourdes until I could appreciate it. Until I was desperate and broken enough to chase healing anywhere, even unto the ends of the earth.

6.

My Faith Is Not Equal
to My Situation

We weren't sure whether Oscar would be willing to sit in a voiture for the entire Mass—he might get restless, and the voiture handles were locked together when parked, rows upon rows. We didn't want to be unable to extricate ourselves gracefully. In truth, Oscar, for the entire duration of the pilgrimage, had displayed exactly one mood: indifferent.

Actually, he was considerably under the weather with a bad cold. About a week before the trip, he had become congested and feverish. The cold before this one had begun like any other, but it ended with an ambulance ride to the hospital to be admitted for pneumonia. Oscar stayed sick that time for nearly three weeks.

So we worried about this new cold surfacing mere days before an international trip. The very day before we left Austin, his pediatrician had signed off on our travel, but Oscar was still stuffy and weak. He had spent most of his time in France so far either asleep or slumped over somebody's shoulder, too tired to hold his head up. He gave no indication that he knew that the shoulder he slumped over was anyplace different than usual. I handed my exhausted, jet-lagged boy to Todd, who laid him gently in his stroller, our compromise for an easier exit. Oscar relaxed, eyes half-mast. The stroller's hood was a near-perfect match for the intense, joyful blue of the voitures that the other malades rode in, and we blended seamlessly back into the stream of people entering the Rosary Basilica.

My first glimpse of the basilica moments before had taken my breath away; I gawked. The entrance stretched in a giant semicircle, and every nook was decorated with mosaics of brilliant color and flashing gold. The extended facade curved around us on both sides, forming a courtyard encircled by long arms. Along the left-hand wall, towering mosaics glowed in the afternoon sun, each depicting one of the five Luminous Mysteries of the Rosary, scenes from Jesus' ministry on earth. The mosaics grew in height as we neared the basilica's grandiose entrance, doors two stories high framed by another shimmering image, depicting the Blessed Mother presenting the rosary to St Dominic. Most of this symbolism was lost on me, as I just admired the beauty of the artwork, not piecing together its meaning or its theme, but overcome with the weight of its glory.

The dizzying effect was multiplied when we entered the interior of the basilica. The high dome soared above us, featuring another mosaic: Mary, just Mary alone, framed by the words *Par Marie a Jesus* (Through Mary to Jesus).

What a fantastic image of Mary!

The entire background of her portrait was an unbroken sea of glittering gold. Her face was strikingly young, even childish. She was neither Middle Eastern nor classical European, but something unexpected and peculiar: unearthly pale, almost translucent, with sharp blue eyes and flaming red hair. The mouth was barely turned up in an expectant half smile (a teenage smirk?). She wore enough jewels and spotted furs to make Marie Antoinette blush, topped off by a crown as tall as her entire head. Her arms spread wide, the better both to embrace you and to show off her unapologetic splendor. The poor, humble mother who laid her child in a dirty manger was nowhere to be found. Here, instead, was the Queen of Heaven and All Angels and Saints. And she was rocking it.

The basilica was packed already. Our stroller transfer and voiture handoff had taken extra time, so Todd and I started to sneak into an open pew near the back, but Kim stopped us. "Follow me. We're moving up."

We made it about halfway to the front of the church, and Kim spotted two Dames she knew well. "I'll ask them to move. They'll do it." There was never ever any arguing with Kim. Todd and I stood awkwardly by while she spoke to the Dames, who immediately stood up and gave their seats to us. We thanked them profusely and settled down to collect ourselves and pray before Mass.

About thirty seconds later, another Dame spotted us and marched over with purposeful strides. "You can't sit back here! You have a malade! All the malades sit up front."

"Oh, but they've already given up their seats for us. We're okay here, really."

"No, you can't see anything from here. Come on."

Feeling more awkward than ever, now that we were abandoning seats that someone had given up on our behalf, we sheepishly (that is to say, with a great deal of embarrassment and as docile as lambs) followed the Dame. I hate being the center of attention. I hate making a fuss. I also hate being told what to do. This crazy parade through the aisles, forcing perfectly comfortable people to move, felt excruciatingly embarrassing. Between the nervous excitement of the trip, my concern for Oscar's health, and our bumbling from seat to seat, I was wound tighter than a drum. My palms began to sweat.

Oscar slept soundly in his stroller in the aisle next to our pew. I locked hands with Todd and rested my head on his shoulder. Carole had joked that this first Lourdes pilgrimage Mass is affectionately called the "Bobblehead Mass," because so many people's heads are lolling as they fight jet lag to stay awake. As much as my nap had refreshed me, my eyes were starting to go blurry again. I wished I had a place to lie down.

The notes of the opening hymn began, one that I had always regarded as slightly cheesy, called "Servant Song." I tried to set aside my snap judgment and embrace the moment. In the universal Church, there is more than one way to be Catholic, more than one type of hymn allowed at Mass. Okay, this one wasn't my favorite. But I was still at Mass in a breathtakingly gorgeous basilica in France, surrounded by more bishops and cardinals than I had fingers and toes. This was probably okay.

"Will you let me be your servant?"[1] As the congregation intoned the hymn, I stiffened. The reflexive bracing was familiar. I did not trust this offer. I did not want or need help. What I wanted was quite simple: for this nightmare not to be true anymore, please and thank you.

But as the earnest words continued—*"We are here to help each other walk the mile and bear the load"*[2]—I abandoned myself to sobbing, maintaining just enough self-awareness to do it quietly. Todd circled me with his arm and pulled me closer, planting a long kiss on the top of my head. The whole, long, hard year of Oscar's illness. All those endless, eternal days of waiting for good news and confronting bad.

All I had wanted, all that time, was not to feel alone. I wanted our son not to be sick, first and foremost. But barring that, I wanted someone to understand what we were going through, to be willing to sit with us in the pain.

That day, as the Order of Malta sang the words I formerly considered so cheesy, I heard the full meaning of the song and the perfect sincerity with which it was offered. They could not cure our son, but they had left their lives behind to accompany us on our pilgrimage, after making it possible in the first place. The precise, military organization; the overwhelming number of doctors and nurses and priests checking on us; the unrelenting insistence that we sit at the front, always—all of it was their way of trying to bear the load.

I felt a profound gratitude, even anticipation. To be sitting in Mass feeling other than skeptical questioning or outright antipathy was a welcome turn. Something long dormant in my heart fluttered. I did not immediately snarl in its direction.

During the homily (the reflection the priest gives after the readings), Archbishop Cordileone of San Francisco asked why people would undertake a pilgrimage at all—not just why we take a pilgrimage, but why we take a pilgrimage *to the site of a Marian apparition.*

When we are facing a difficult time in our lives, said Archbishop Cordileone, and we are a person of faith, it's natural to reach a point where we think to ourselves: "My faith is not equal to my situation."

My faith is not equal to my situation.

In a handful of words, he had captured my spiritual reality, as precisely as a butterfly pinned under glass.

He continued, "In finding our own faith insufficient, we come to this place to draw on Mary's faith."

The members of the Order of Malta were here to carry the load of my physical and emotional burdens.

Mary, he explained, was here to make up for the load of my insufficient faith.

Until this point, I hadn't realized that my insufficient faith had been an almost equally heavy, scary burden. As a Christian, times of suffering are what we are built for, right? What did my reaction say about me when my faith seemed to crumble before this challenge?

It said that I was human. It said that the Church had an answer for me already: my faith is not equal, but Mary's always was and always is.

7.

On Holding On and Letting Go

By the time Mass ended, Oscar was fast asleep in the stroller, and our voiture and charioteer had gone missing outside the basilica. It took an absurd amount of time for our pod to locate all its members. Todd and I brought Oscar into the courtyard, where we bumped into Amy but couldn't find anyone else. In a flashback to those woebegone years before smartphones and instant communication, we had to form a search plan and choose someone to stay put as a landmark. Once we reunited, Ryan received another dressing-down for misplacing the voiture. Kim imposed the penance of demotion from pulling the honored voiture to pushing the stroller where Oscar slept on, unmindful of our comedy of errors.

Todd and I followed, hands joined. As we walked, Todd finally circled back to the conversation he had had during my afternoon nap. The Knight from Hugh's team had recounted a story that afternoon on the patio about an experience from a previous pilgrimage.

One year, the Knight had told them, a woman who came to Lourdes was on dialysis and in near complete kidney failure. She required a lot of complicated electrical equipment to keep her alive and could only walk very short distances without tiring. She was also very, very angry. She was angry about her life and about her dependence on these machines. She was mistrustful of the pilgrimage and of the course of her illness. What time she did not spend complaining, she spent putzing with her machinery, babying it, double-checking the settings. Of course, she participated in the various pilgrimage activities, but her soul was not there with her, only the albatross of her equipment and its routines. She was constantly distracted by the many mechanisms of control she had set up for her life to be successful (which is to say, prolonged as a slave to her machinery).

According to the Knight's story, at some point the malade's machinery broke. The woman spent the rest of the pilgrimage furious that she had been put in such a position, unable to believe that things could fall apart to such an extent. How could God let this happen? She had upended her life to step out in trust on pilgrimage, and her lifesaving medical equipment was useless to her.

Her team reassured her. "We are doing everything we can to find the parts you need. How do you feel?"

"Actually," she snapped, "I feel fine. Better than I have in months."

Her dialysis equipment was fixed. But for the duration of her trip, she was so bitter about the whole experience, she hardly noticed that she could walk much further, that her energy and color had improved. By the time she returned home, her doctor informed her that she had been healed to the point that she no longer needed a kidney transplant. And finally her eyes were opened, and she awakened to her own misjudgment. She had refused to surrender her pride, or her machinery, or her insistence on her dependence and control.

God healed her anyway.

Our healing doesn't come through our own efforts, heroic and technologically advanced as those may be. It comes always, and only, at the will of God. Clinging tightly to the things of this world, pulling all the levers we can pull: none of it matters. In some cases, we learn this through personal failure, hitting wall after wall before we realize our utter dependence on God. In her case, she learned it through spectacular and gratuitous success.

I listened to this entire story, my hand in Todd's. Though our bodies moved in pace, separated by only inches, the gulf between us grew and grew as he spoke. My face turned to stone and my hand in his to lead.

"Why are you telling me this?" (Bitchy wife translation: "In what way do you think I am failing you and Oscar? Why do you think *I* am like that woman?")

He responded softly, "She couldn't let go. She couldn't surrender to the experience of the pilgrimage. She felt as if she had to control everything in order for healing to happen."

Silence.

"Hugh's wife has inoperable lung cancer. They have three girls."

Louder silence.

"I just—I know you're anxious. I'm trying to say that you don't have to be. Things are going to happen here that you don't expect and can't predict, but you have to let them. You have to get out of your own way. You have to get out of God's way."

Since Oscar's diagnosis, I had devoted most of the time formerly spent praying to perfecting my newest hobby: being a professional special-needs parent. I begged a neurology textbook from the nurses at the hospital and pored through it with macabre fascination. I disappeared down rabbit trails of scholarly publications, clicking through PubMed until my eyes watered. I created accounts on message boards dedicated to epilepsy and developmental delays, swapping stories during the eerie midnight hours of one hospital stay after another.

My obsessive research created even more tension in our marriage, which was already under stress from the incessant demands of six young kids, an unfinished 150-year-old house, and Todd's high-pressure, travel-heavy job. From the moment Oscar got sick, Todd and I approached the medical situation in extremely different ways. Where I had a gnawing, insatiable need to figure out exactly what was going on in the most painstaking detail possible, Todd faced the days with no small measure of incuriosity. I wanted to game out all the endless variations and chart a ready course of action for each one. For his part, Todd listened closely to our doctors; after some clarifying and probing questions, he accepted their recommendations at face value. More than once, he flatly refused to listen to something that my endless hours of research had uncovered. "What's the point of getting worked up about that? Why don't we just wait and see what the doctors say?"

"The doctors aren't always right. They don't *know* everything—especially with kids whose situations are unique. *We* are the experts on Oscar. And they've already missed a lot of things and made some calls that I don't think were the right ones. *We* have to be his advocates, because if we don't do it, who *will*?" My voice grew shriller and more panicky with each sentence.

With infuriating gentleness, he spoke to me as if speaking to a patient in a psychiatric ward, which is where my anxiety and I probably belonged. "But you don't know either, Christy. These are all just possibilities."

"Don't you want to even know what the possibilities are?" I shot back accusingly.

"No, not really. I just want to take care of Oscar, figure out what he needs today. There is absolutely no way to predict what's going to happen tomorrow, and I have too much other stuff going on to waste energy trying to do that. I have work to do. The house is falling apart. The other kids need us." I could tell he was upset now, upset in that quiet way he has. Todd rarely raises his voice; he grows somehow both increasingly restless and increasingly reasonable. He reached across and took my hands in his, trying to meet my downcast eyes with his seaside, blue-green-gray ones. I didn't look because I knew I would lose my own self-righteous footing in those eyes.

Todd's love language is touch; he is always seeking physical connection. (Six kids, y'all.) He is also extremely empathic, furiously laying down one paving stone after another as he tries to make common ground with anyone and everyone, but especially with me. I knew this routine: this argument was going the way of so many arguments before. He was handling me, and I did not want to be handled.

"I'm not saying you're wrong to do this," he persisted, evenly, gingerly. "I know that this is part of who you are and how you engage in the world. It's one of the things I love about you. You throw yourself into things completely. But I don't think you're doing yourself or Oscar any favors right now. I won't stop you, but I wish you would stop yourself."

I didn't want to be met where I was. I wanted to win. I wanted everyone in the world, but especially in this house, to be as upset as I was, in the way that I was. Not to be wailing and gnashing teeth and rending garments, but to be opening door after door after door in relentless research. To not quit until we, through unbridled determination, uncovered the one hidden, cutting-edge, scientific advance that would cure our unfixable son. Stop myself? No. I fought back against my compassionate, hurting husband, the most effective way I knew how: I pulled my hands out of his, turned my stony face to the door, and walked away.

I endured countless appointments and therapy sessions with Oscar by myself during Todd's workdays. They were often ones where I would bear the brunt of bad news or hold up one end of a heavy conversation. Over and over, each new doctor apologetically downgraded the long-term outlook. (That I brought these heavy conversations on myself by asking pointed, unanswerable questions did not escape my own notice. I had to *know*.)

I resented that Todd wasn't there to hold my hand in one beige office after another, and I resented that I had to reexperience it each time I came home to explain the results. I resented even more that he seemed unperturbed, resigned. He was not unaffected; he *cared*. But he did not carry those cares around his neck like a millstone, as I did. He shrugged and sighed, saying, "The Lord gives, and the Lord takes away."

And in my anger and pain and utter confusion at this perfectly reasonable (and equally pained) response, I retreated. My extroverted husband, who needs to talk things out to process and understand them, had no one to talk to. Forget physical affection—we weren't even sleeping in the same room anymore. Oscar's frequent night-waking meant that we took turns, one with Oscar, one getting a solid eight hours in another room. Our silence and the space between us propped up an uneasy truce, a marital demilitarized zone.

I wasn't just upset that Todd wasn't in sync with me on the research side. I was consumed with jealousy that his faith seemed undisturbed. *How*, I thought to myself, *can he just sit there and continue to pray as if nothing has happened?*

He was completely broken, too, in his own way. If I had bothered to look, I would have seen that he was wearing his suffering on his sleeve—or rather, on his face. Todd had grown a beard during the year, one that I assumed was a passive-aggressive manifestation of the distance between us. (I had never liked beards.) One day, a friend asked why he had grown it.

Todd answered, "It's because of Oscar."

I did a double take. He went on to explain that he had stopped shaving during one of Oscar's early hospital visits, trying to cut precious minutes from his daily routine. And then he just kept not shaving. It became a kind of penance, a continuous offering, a dying to himself. He shrugged, "It's just not time to shave it off yet. I don't know when that will be. But I feel like I'm waiting for . . . something."

My husband had been wearing this "hair shirt" for months, and I hadn't noticed.

I had shut myself off so effectively that I was routinely surprised to discover, as in this instance, that Todd was suffering—and he was dealing with it alone, for the most part, because I had little to offer anyone, including myself. Frank Deford, in his memoir honoring the life and death of his daughter, Alex, from cystic fibrosis, described similar challenges with his wife. "The problem was that each of us needed to draw the same consolation from each other," he recounts. "How, in desperation—guilty, angry, frustrated, scared—how could I turn for solace to my wife, the mother of my child, when she was the mother of the child dying, and going through all the same as I, wanting the same thing I did? How do you give the very thing you need more of yourself?"[1]

It wasn't until much, much later, months after Lourdes, that I began to unpack the hell my husband had lived through. He told me, "Sure, I relinquished control to God. What else could I do? But I was also thinking to myself, 'And this is all it is.' There was no joy in it at all."

"That still sounds easier than fury and despair," I replied.

"I don't know. Resignation is dangerous in its own way. I was lukewarm. I was not grateful for anything God had given me, least of all Oscar. *Whatever. This is it.* There was no room in my mind for mercy."

Our silence spoke volumes, but not to each other. I withdrew. Todd soldiered on blankly. Day after day, I broke my husband's heart, and he broke mine, and Oscar broke both.

We had arrived back at our sister hotels for dinner. I was more than ready for a stiff drink and to introduce a buffer between myself and my husband—as well as between myself and myself.

Mingling, however, is not my forte. I am a fan of neither small talk nor strangers, but I *am* a fan of French wine. After procuring a glass, slamming it down, and procuring a second, I scanned the room. Kim waved me over to a table she had claimed and introduced me to Pete Weber, a doctor and member of the medical team.

"What kind of doctor are you?"

"I'm a cardiologist. I'm from Duluth."

"Oh, we lived in Minnesota for a year! Is this your first time on pilgrimage?"

"No. I was here last year as a malade."

I blinked. I wasn't sure, at first, where to go to with that. Was it okay to ask why? Whether he was still sick? He was a wiry man—was he wasting away? Were his bright eyes and cheeks from pleasure or pathology? These questions crossed my mind every time I met a new malade, but I was taken aback to find a prior malade hidden among the volunteers. I groped for a new approach.

"I bet it's different being here as a volunteer. I know we are only one day in, but what have you noticed so far?"

Pete leaned across the table, intimate and earnest. "Oh, it's *completely* different. Like night and day. Let me tell you one thing I wish someone had told me at the beginning of my last trip. The key is to *surrender* to the experience."

That word again.

He continued, "At home, caregivers are overwhelmed with the decisions they have to make every day. There are so many details, medical decisions on top of everyday ones, and you work so hard not to let anything slip through the cracks. Everything completely depends on you, and it's totally exhausting.

"You don't have any decisions to make here. Literally none. You don't have to decide where you're staying, or what to eat, or where to go next. You have to surrender to all the things that have been arranged for you. And that's purposeful."

He spoke as if delivering a finished oration, oblivious to my silence. He'd been ruminating on this, I realized. "All of those decisions have been handled—taken away from you, in fact—to make space. Space for you to have an encounter. When your mind is full of clutter, you can't encounter Christ. You have to let go."

My head was pounding, trying to process this revelation. What Pete had said was upending my carefully tended and nurtured facade of total self-sufficiency and control, which I had dutifully carried with me all the way to France. But even though I was already reeling, he wasn't finished.

"The other side of the coin is that the malade's job is to allow the Knights and Dames to do their job so they can have *their* pilgrimage. They are here to serve, and they can't do that if you don't let them. If you fight for control, you are denying them the joy of serving Christ by serving you."

Boom.

Ask me to surrender my pride and independence for my own sake, and I would nod and smile and tighten my clutch, resolute that things would only go well if I micromanaged the details. But he had pointed out that my control issues were hurting other people, these people I had already come to like and admire for their selflessness. Dampen *their* pilgrimage experience by refusing to let them take care of Oscar? That I couldn't abide.

This was not my own selflessness coming to the fore here, sadly; it was my need not to make a mistake or screw anything up. Perfectionism was the story of my life. But if I was going to be perfect at anything, if I could control just *one* thing, I would control myself.

I would be a perfectly submissive pilgrim.

8.

PROSTRATE IN THE MUD

I woke up the next morning with that complete bodily and mental confusion that heralds the arrival of your first sunrise in a new country. Oscar was cooing quietly in his crib. Todd was gone. As the early riser in our marriage, he had long since perfected the habit of sneaking out of the room quietly to grab a cup of coffee, filling the hours before his wife decides to face the world.

When I reached down to lift Oscar, I froze.

His entire lower face, nose to chin, was crusted with an enormous black scab, with patches of oozy red. It looked like he had been physically attacked in the night. He gazed up at me with perfect equanimity; juxtaposing his calm repose with the bloody mess of his face, I had a sudden chilling sense of the diabolical, some demon-haunted closet stuffed with giggling Beelzebubs just nearby.

I picked him up quickly and was even more perturbed to realize that his clothes and sheets were all completely clean—not a trace of blood on anything but his face. *He must have had a nosebleed overnight. Probably all the changes in air between the plane and the mountains. It must have been oozing very slowly for a long time*, I reassured myself. Still, the effect was troubling. Foreboding enshrouded me like gray mist.

I already would have been off-balance without waking to find a blood-soaked baby where I had left my cherubic son the night before.

Today, we would take Oscar to the baths, he would receive the sacrament of healing, and we would participate in Lourdes's famous candlelight Rosary procession. These three events are the main attractions Lourdes has to offer, piled up during our first full day on the ground. At JFK airport before departure, an anticipatory shiver had rattled me when I had browsed our orientation packet and seen the blockbuster schedule for this day. I had thought, that distant moment 48 hours ago, "That's it. That's the day our son will be healed, or he won't. By the end of that day, we will know whether God has granted us our miracle."

Oh, how little I believed. (*Help my unbelief!*)

I had fought not to succumb to this simplistic if-this-then-that theology, but I could not disengage the mindset that God either would or would not answer our prayer—and that his answer would reveal how he really felt about us. I knew, intellectually, that this wasn't true. I knew all the theological explanations about how when God says no to our prayer, it's because he has something better in mind for us.

But all of our prayers, since the day of Oscar's first seizure—all the big and little things we had asked for since then—had been subjugated beneath the One Prayer to Rule Them All: *God, please heal my son.* In fact, all those other prayers, and all the secret, truest parts of my soul, had been hidden behind the barricade of that one prayer. *I'm asking today for help with balancing all the tasks in my life as a mother, God. Please help me to do your will . . . but we both know that if you really loved me, you would heal my son.* I wielded that prayer like a weapon, clung to it like the bomb detonator in a hostage negotiation. *If you don't heal my son, I won't love you anymore, and it's impossible that you love me.*

As far as my soul was concerned, Oscar was the means to an end. If my prayer was the bomb detonator, Oscar was quite literally the human shield.

Once again, we processed from our hotel to the Domain, about a ten-minute walk across the river and through bouncy cobbled streets. Delivery trucks rattled along at our heels, and the scents of yeast and sugar and chocolate wafted around every corner. Todd was with Oscar in the voiture, which allowed me to stand back and observe the entire spectacle with some detachment—a vaguely hostile detachment, given the state of my mind that morning. I had wanted so badly to come to

Lourdes with openness and no expectations. I wanted it so badly that I had deliberately not studied anything about what would happen on our trip. I read no guidebooks, bought no maps, and only glanced at the materials the Order of Malta sent us—just enough to figure out how to get ourselves to the plane. My intent was to surrender and turn myself over to whatever was going to happen.

That morning, though, surrender seemed impossible. Every ounce of anger and confusion toward God that I had wrestled against all year nestled itself around my shoulders and threatened to choke me. I was still resentful about the story Todd had shared the night before about the woman on dialysis, because I saw so much of myself in her haughty, jittery need for control. I hated myself for that, and I wanted so badly not to be her, but I had no idea how to free myself. With each step, my legs felt heavier and my arms tightened around my chest. I was so tired of being hurt, and I could not bear to be hurt anymore. I could not bear for one more dream to be crushed, one more avenue to healing closed.

All around me, people were chatting and laughing. I withdrew, thinking scornfully about what an absurd little parade we were. What was there to be so full of joyful anticipation about? Had we actually flown to France to touch some dirty water from an overcrowded spring in the hopes that it would have some impact on the way our baby's neurons fired? That idea was patently nuts. My cheeks burned with embarrassment.

Why were we even here?

Long before our departure, I knew this pilgrimage was going to either make or break my faith. I feared, even expected, that it would break. "God, this is your last chance," I told him bluntly. "I don't believe that you can fix either my son or my faith." I thought that, yet I remained desperate to be proven wrong! The possibility that I was right—that God was absent or uncaring or nonexistent—was too terrible to contemplate. The alternative, that he was not absent but still wouldn't do anything to redeem this unholy mess, was incomprehensible.

I had run face-first and at full speed into the wall of that immortal question: How can a benevolent God allow suffering in the world?

I spent the quiet hours after the children went to bed, hours I should have spent sleeping, grappling with other theologians and their response to the problem of pain. "Not that I am (I think) in much danger of ceasing to believe in God," wrote C. S. Lewis in *A Grief Observed*, a painfully frank meditation on the death of his wife. "The real danger is of coming to believe such dreadful things about Him. The conclusion I dread is not 'So there's no God after all,' but 'So this is what God's really like. Deceive yourself no longer.'"[1]

Our family life was a high-wire act, a precarious and precise feat of schedule engineering. People saw me making it on time to school, six children dressed and homework in tow. Sometimes their socks even matched. They saw me shuffling Oscar to and from therapy and appointments, lining up babysitters with military discipline, showing up for parish functions and smiling amiably.

What they did not see: me sobbing uncontrollably on the floor of my bedroom at two o'clock in the afternoon. Me clicking away on the internet, researching one more rare disease research study Oscar might qualify for, while my toddler tugged at my sleeve asking for a glass of milk. Me calling my parents, tight anxiety poorly disguised in my voice, and them showing up at the door twenty minutes later to whisk the kids off for a sleepover. My five oldest children screaming at each other unsupervised, chasing each other with sticks, and generally trashing the house, while I closed the door and rocked Oscar on my shoulder, wishing it all, all, all away.

It had not been a beautiful year.

I spent an inordinate amount of time and energy putting a sunny spin on my answer to the inevitable, awkward question posed by everyone I met: *How's Oscar?* It was an in-passing kind of question, and there was no proper in-passing kind of answer except the false, one-note, blindly optimistic one. *Seizures are controlled! He is fat and happy! We sure are lucky to have this cross. How can we offer it up for you?*

I wonder now whether the censorship was something I imposed upon myself. Possibly my friends did want real answers. During a spiritual talk, one month prior, I had suffered a complete emotional breakdown surrounded by friends from my parish—the only time in those twelve months when I had involuntarily forfeited my mask. These remarkable women rallied without hesitation, with their words and their outstretched arms, like an army arrayed for battle with the purest shining love, polished and gleaming.

Then again, I vividly remember a day when I ran into an acquaintance, moments after Oscar had had a seizure in the backseat of the car as I drove. (It was an ordinary afternoon, a regular Tuesday. I stopped to check and console him, then continued my errands.) She hugged me hello and asked (wait for it!), "How's Oscar?" The tears I had been tamping down into a growing boulder at the top of my throat leapt into my eyes instantly. I gasped and pressed my lips together. She glanced at me, startled, and then pityingly. "Oh, you still have tears?" she murmured. The disentanglement from that moment was clumsy and graceless for both of us.

While I perfected my phony cheerleader routine, Oscar endured daily seizures of multiple types, including one bluntly categorized by the medical establishment as "catastrophic." Six drugs failed to stop them before the seventh worked, though it carried a black-box FDA warning label and only worked in combination with an intense diet requiring us to weigh and balance everything he ate or drank, to the tenth of a gram. At an age when most children are toddling around and picking up new words by the dozens, we coaxed and cajoled Oscar to pull himself six feet across a padded mat, an effort that left him sweaty and red-faced. Every new month, he missed a new milestone; the list of all the ways he failed to meet society's unyielding demands to be "normal" and "typical" extended in lengthening, emotionless, black-and-white rows down countless pages of clinic notes. He made eye contact and smiled readily, but he was unnervingly quiet, cooing lightly in response to talking, crying only when he was tired or hungry, laughing rarely.

Oscar was so much more to us than his medical challenges. He was a joy to be around because he demanded so little; he peered deeply into our eyes, straight down to the purest parts of our souls. He was satisfied with himself as he was and with the world as it was. Despite his lack of worldly progress, Oscar maintained a supernatural tranquility, peace radiating outward from him in a wide pool so immersive that it was nearly visible.

Whenever my parents visited, my father would gather Oscar into his arms, then settle into our recliner, crossing his ankle over his opposite knee and propping the baby into the crook. They would sit that way for an hour or more, gazing at each other with goofy smiles and perfect love. Oscar had that effect on everyone, melting them into puddles of meaningless cooing and caresses. Only he and Grandpa, though, seemed to ascend together to a private mountaintop and commune, heedless of everyone else in the room.

I maintained my own existence on the brink—superficial equilibrium versus hidden despair, the quiet joy of being Oscar's mother against the loss of my imagined future for him, my simmering inward rage repudiating the placid outward practice of my faith—as long as I could. I couldn't admit, even to myself, the naked truths about my sadness, the unconfessed ableism that was its bedrock: I loved my son's smiles, but I wanted even more to hear him say, "Mama." I breathed in the delicious scent of his chubby neck, but I wanted even more to breathe in a fistful of wildflowers that he brought me from our front yard. I wanted more for him. He was not enough, as he was. Lourdes was his last and only hope, and God's last and only chance with me.

By the time we reached the St. Joseph Gate, I pulled myself together enough to resume conversation. I began chatting with Amy Cattapan, the late addition to Oscar's pod. This was her first pilgrimage to Lourdes too. She wasn't a natural leader like Kim, or a socialite like Carole, or a networker like Ryan—she studied the place and the people, her keen eyes darting from place to place beneath her curly hair (the kind of unfrizzy ringlets that I always aspired to but never quite got). Her gifts of observation and intuition served her well in her career as a writer.

"Your kids might enjoy my last book, *7 Riddles to Nowhere*. It's about a boy who goes on a scavenger hunt to win a prize that will save his Catholic school," Amy explained. "The story is very dear to me—a school where I used to work was closed down. Writing that book was a way for me to process what happened by writing an alternate ending."

The appeal of writing an alternate ending? I could relate. So could every malade and caregiver in a five-mile radius.

We had made our way across the plaza of the Domain and assembled before an interesting building (and that is the nicest applicable adjective). The Church of St. Bernadette, a modernist, concrete imposition on the landscape, was erected at the site of the last apparition of the Blessed Mother to St. Bernadette, across the river from the grotto where she first appeared. It was an uninspiring edifice: utilitarian, solid, blocky.

The inside was no better—hard, reverberating floors; plain, wooden bleachers; musty, frigid air. The color scheme made liberal use of harvest yellows and oranges, with some troubling accents of lavender. The walls seemed to be made of pleated beige curtains. There were no windows, but light poured in through the exterior doors and the ceiling skylights, broken by a spiderweb of metal struts. The altar supports were molded concrete boulders. A massive, traditional pipe organ lined the entire back wall.

It was a very confusing aesthetic. I felt as if we had been transported to some liminal, otherworldly place, separated from both the bustle of the real world and the almost overpowering beauty of the rest of the Domain outside. It was like a time capsule, or an interplanetary holding area.

As usual, the voitures carrying the malades were lined up and locked together in the open space in front. Every church was designed to accommodate the malades in a place of honor. One of the many priests surrounding the altar brought out a monstrance and exposed the Blessed Sacrament, the consecrated host in its center. The congregation, almost in unison, hit their knees on the pebbly concrete. Even several of the malades, the more mobile ones, stepped out of their voitures and knelt beside them.

After opening hymns and prayers, we began a Rosary. Most of the pilgrims seated themselves again. Todd remained resolutely kneeling, though, and I stayed down in solidarity with him. We were praying through the five Sorrowful Mysteries, the five crucial moments of Christ's passion and death on the Cross. The first decade is Christ's Agony in the Garden, where he prayed so hard to be spared from death that his sweat fell from him like drops of blood. That was a prayer we were all living, every moment of every day.

After the first mystery, a priest stepped forward to offer the first of several reflection talks. The pebbles were grinding painfully into my knees, and I sat. Todd continued kneeling.

"It is only when Bernadette is willing to get down in the dirt, to let go of all the things big people cling to and lower herself so completely that she is prostrate in the mud, that God makes the waters flow with a superabundance of his grace." The priest's voice was heavy and slow, an invocation.

"When you have humbled and emptied yourself of everything you cling to—your plans, your dreams, your pride, your sins, your successes—when you have emptied yourself of everything that you think belongs to you, God fills up that emptiness."

So much easier said than done. I had longed for that fullness of God's grace, scratched and scraped for it. All along, insisted this priest, the secret was to stop fighting. Drop your weapons. Open your hands. Empty your heart. Confession was one of the keys to this emptiness, he concluded. When God absolves us through the priest, he "cleans out our hearts to make room for the grace which is his presence in our lives."

It was clear now why this reflection was the first spiritual pep talk we had received in Lourdes. If we couldn't get step one right, if we couldn't empty ourselves, then nothing else that followed would take root and bear fruit. God's grace couldn't work in us, as long as we were holding on to our wills instead of his.

The invitation was clear: *surrender.*

During the rest of the Rosary and two more reflection talks, we were invited to step out of the crowd for Confession. Somewhere around the second decade, when I spotted an opening, I stepped to the right-hand wall.

"Bless me, Father, for I have sinned. It's been about a month since my last Confession . . . ," I began, not knowing where to begin. I talked about why we were in Lourdes, about Oscar and his seizures, about how I feared for his health and harbored anger at God. I talked about how I did these things so often that they felt like safety blankets—I reveled in my fear and anger. And suddenly I couldn't stop listing all the things I was fearful and angry about.

Confession, Catholics are often told, is not therapy. You are supposed to say your sins, as well as the number of times you have committed each, and to brook no excuses or explanations or finger-pointing. But that day, I found it impossible to tell my sins without telling the stories behind each, and then the stories behind those stories. One expanded into another, like blood draining out of a murder victim into an ever-widening puddle that would only stop when the heart stopped beating.

I talked until I was nearly breathless, uninterrupted.

The priest, an elderly monsignor, waited a few beats before he spoke. He gazed at me. I couldn't read the thoughts behind his eyes.

Finally, he said, in the most tender voice imaginable, "You are carrying a lot of sorrow."

I yelped a teary, shaky laugh, a single note.

He probed gently with his next questions, but he neither condemned nor accused. That Confession was handled with kid gloves. Never, in any Confession before or since, have I been more certain that Jesus was speaking to me directly through the priest.

"For your penance, say one Hail Mary." He said the words of absolution, and my empty heart lifted.

9.

GETHSEMANE

After lunch on Friday, barely twenty-four hours after touching down in France, we began our third procession of the trip, the *big one*: we were going to the baths. I listened through jet-lagged haze as our charioteer, Ryan, chattered happily away about everything and nothing, laughing and joking. I don't remember what he was talking about. I remember being enraged that he couldn't telepathically sense my skyrocketing agitation. How could he not smell turmoil seeping out of my pores?

The pivotal moment we had prayed and hoped and planned for was finally happening. Our son had come to be healed in the waters of Lourdes . . . or not.

I was deathly silent, trying to block out Ryan's relentlessly cheerful small talk as my hands itched to slap him, my legs tensed to sprint away. My throat constricted, my ears roared, and my breath came in ragged, shallow bursts. Ryan stopped talking midthought and, without missing a beat, started praying over us smoothly, as if he had been doing that all along.

"Holy Spirit, I ask you to come and bless this family. Give them your peace and security. Blessed Mother, let them know how much you love them; let them feel your mantle wrapped around them. We ask your healing for Oscar, and for Todd and Christy to be open to this experience and whatever it holds for them."

He continued for a minute or more, praying almost as quickly and intently as he had been talking moments ago. As he prayed, my chest stopped heaving and the roar inside my head fell still. By the time we reached the last footbridge to turn toward the baths, I had nearly recollected myself from fiend back to human. Our pod lapsed into companionable silence.

Oscar was lethargic, his eyes vacant, halfway between waking and sleeping. Todd seemed unaware of the menacing floodwaters of my staggering anxiety—or (more likely) I was too smothered by that anxiety to perceive whatever he was feeling, to offer him even the smallest blessing of a word, a smile, a hand. When we neared the front of the line, I lifted Oscar and his head fell limply, fully surrendered to sleep. Because men, women, and mothers with children each have separate bathing areas, Oscar would go with me into the children's baths, while Todd would go alone the other way.

As soon as I reached the front of the line, the entrance gate to the main waiting area was snapped shut before me by a *hospitaller*, a Lourdes volunteer trained to keep pilgrims flowing smoothly through the busy sanctuary. My mind warred between rage and panic, feeling as if we had been denied entry, before I realized that it wasn't personal. They had simply paused the line while prayers began. Even after I understood, distrust roiled in my breast, leaching into every heartbeat to contaminate the farthest cells of my fingertips.

Bells began pealing, echoing as if the rock walls of the grotto were springing to life. A man inside the closed-off waiting area chanted the "Regina Coeli," and the familiar words and melody washed the heat out of my chest in an ebbing wave. *Regina Coeli, laetare, alleluia! Queen of Heaven, rejoice, alleluia!*

As soon as the last words were sung (*Pray for us to God, alleluia!*), the hospitaller opened the gate and gestured us forward. At the last second before we entered the baths, the entire assembly begged Mary to pray to God on our behalf. I liked the properness of beginning at the beginning: the opening of the gate and our first steps inside lined up neatly with the opening prayers of the Rosary, which was chanted in continuous loops all day, every day. *I believe in God*, my right foot began. *The Father almighty*, my left agreed. They led my head and my heart, which contained beliefs about which I was far less certain.

Todd moved left, to the men's side. As I turned right, another hospitaller raced over and waved both his hands, palms out, for me to stop. He and the first hospitaller began to converse rapidly in a foreign language. The knots of prayer holding me together, those small balms from a heartbeat before, came undone. I stood in front of a crowd of praying and waiting pilgrims, holding my child's limp body, heat rising in my cheeks, while the men argued. The second man grudgingly let us pass, and we turned to cross to the children's baths.

Five paces later a third hospitaller stopped us, with furrowed brows for me and whispered, angry, foreign words for the man I was following. He jabbed his finger sharply at the podium where a priest was leading the Rosary.

I blinked hard, refusing to cry. I was clueless about how this was supposed to go; in line, Carole had told me to just trust myself to the hospitallers, who would take care of everything. These hospitallers could not agree on a plan, though. They argued in words I couldn't understand, before a crowd of pilgrims doing their best to pray composedly and ignore the commotion. I had dreamed of this day for months. This humiliating argument had no place in those dreams. After what felt like an eternity, the last man grudgingly stepped aside and waved us past with a harrumph. I stepped forward obediently on shaky legs before he could change his mind.

At the doorway to the children's baths, there was an empty short bench to the left, with a longer bench to the right, where many mothers and children were already waiting to enter. The hospitaller gestured that I should sit on the empty left-hand bench alone, apart from the others.

I sat with an uncertain glance at all the people to the right. A female hospitaller ushered out a mother and child who had just finished bathing, then turned to the right-hand bench and took the next person in line, as if she hadn't noticed me and Oscar at all. I felt certain now that I was in the wrong place—the wrong bench, the wrong country.

The Rosary leader announced, in English, the first Sorrowful Mystery, the Agony in the Garden, when Jesus prayed to God the Father to let the coming suffering and death pass him by. Tears slid down my cheeks, the small anxious tears of this awkward moment, of frustration and uncertainty, of mishandling of steps and wrong places in line. But also, of course, there were the larger tears. Our Lord's plea had become our plea—*Let this cup pass us by. Heal our son.* (And the part I always, always choked on: *Yet not my will but yours be done.*) This sturdy bench was my Gethsemane.

This significant moment also carried potent timing: the following day marked the anniversary of Oscar's first seizure. I mourned the loss of the woman I had been a year ago. I mourned her carefree, untested faith.

In front of us, rows of female pilgrims sat on identical wooden benches, fingering their beads, moving their lips, waiting to enter the women's baths. Many were also watching me and the other mothers with children, as we sat against the wall. I glanced at the women on the other side of the door, some of whom had more than one child with them. I wondered what had brought them to Lourdes. I wondered whether what had brought them was worse than what had brought me.

The hospitaller brought in another family from the right-hand bench, then looked at me, eyes widening. She looked at the woman on the right, then back at me in dawning realization. She tried to ask us both who was next, in a language neither of us spoke. We looked helplessly at each other and shrugged mutely at the doorkeeper.

She indicated to me that I would be next. I looked at the other mother, and she nodded and smiled, gesturing to the curtained door. I acquiesced. Truthfully, I felt entitled: Oscar was much younger than her child. But mostly, I felt selfish and greedy for something to go right, to be easy.

Across the crowd of seated women, the waiting line of voitures from our pilgrimage group still extended down the road. I made eye contact with Donna, Hugh's wife, a mother with a doting husband, three beautiful daughters, and Stage IV lung cancer. She was watching me openly, her head cocked, her gaze full of love and pity. I watched her watching us, Oscar and I composing a miniature Pietà. Here I sat, the sorrowful mother, holding the body of my suffering son, begging for God's mercy. I felt no satisfaction in this, only grim recognition of my powerlessness to control the outcome. Mary wasn't spared. Why should I be?

A minute passed, or perhaps an hour. A mother and child came out with a hospitaller, who turned and beckoned to me. I stood, Oscar snoring quietly on my shoulder, and walked behind the curtain.

We entered a small changing area. Directly in front of me, a second curtain separating the dressing area from the baths stood wide open. In this lower section stood two baths, the first about knee high and eight feet long, the other smaller, raised to waist height, obviously meant for children.

In the farthest corner stood a volunteer. Our eyes locked.

Kim.

Our Kim. Oscar's pod host Kim. Good old, take-charge, indomitable Kim.

If I had not been wired with tension, I might have collapsed with relief.

The woman at the door greeted me: "Italiano?" I said, "English," very stupidly—ugly American!—and she gracefully switched to English, speaking with a lilting accent I couldn't place. She took Oscar from my arms and laid him on a changing table, beginning to undress him.

The foreign woman at the door was clearly in charge. She gently held my elbow and said, "For babies, we don't put them in the bath; we do it this way." She reached underneath the changing table and pulled out a shallow green bowl, made of plastic, full of water. She dipped her fingers and lifted a few drops. "The baths are so cold. This is the same water from the spring, and we just put some over his head while you say your prayers. It's very beautiful."

Just a moment ago I had very clearly seen a small, child-sized, actual bath.

Instead, they offered my son Tupperware.

While my mind, body, and soul had all parted ways at the door, my logic reasserted itself. I was quite sure we had not come all the way to France for Oscar to be sprinkled from a bowl.

Out of the corner of my eye, I glanced at Kim uncertainly. She shook her head, almost imperceptibly.

Emboldened, I said flatly, "No. He's going in the bath."

The woman in charge acquiesced graciously. They asked me to start undressing myself on the other side of the room. A third volunteer held a large blue blanket up for modesty while I shook and fumbled with zippers and clasps. To calm me, they made gentle conversation and asked the baby's name. "Oscar," I replied robotically, struggling to fold my pants and wondering what to do with them. *Hang them? Lay them on the chair? Should I hide my underwear in the pocket?*

Another woman, an American, turned around swiftly. "Oh, this is Oscar? The doctors are very worried about seizures. They don't want him in the bath because it's so cold."

Almost without my conscious will, I answered again, in monotone. "He's going in the bath. His seizures are not related to temperature or sensory issues."

I was shaking by this point from the numerous confrontations, added to the pile of anxiety that had been mounting all afternoon. I continued undressing, slowly and clumsily. Even though I was fully shielded by the blanket, I felt so exposed, so stupid, so sure, suddenly, that I had approached this whole experience incorrectly. I had interrupted the Rosary; I sat in the wrong place; I couldn't even be polite or decide what to do with my underwear. What if I was wrong about Oscar's bath too?

When I was finally unclothed, the volunteer wrapped me in the blue towel, and the American who had been tending Oscar handed him to Kim. They helped me down the steps between the two baths, and Kim guided me toward the little children's bath. It was a concrete rectangle about the size of a crib, holding water eight inches deep.

Kim touched my shoulder gently. "Take a moment to recollect yourself and think of your intentions. We'll wait until you're ready."

I stood there blankly. Not a single thought was in my head. I had neither words nor tears to spare for this moment. How had I not prepared? I finally managed to pray lamely in my heart: *Please heal my son.*

I wasn't sure anymore what that meant, or whether it mattered. Why could I not accept this child as he was? What kind of mother was I, so dissatisfied with a gift that I crossed an entire ocean to beg for an exchange? Was I literally asking for him to stand up and climb out of the bath, to reach for me and say, "Mama"? Did I believe that was possible?

Why was I even here?

I nodded to Kim; we turned to face the bath. As she lifted Oscar away from her body, I removed his diaper, and another volunteer removed his blue towel and replaced it with a white sheet, wet with cold water from the bath. Oscar whimpered and squealed.

I had held him down, ignoring his pitiful cries, for countless medical procedures because I understood their purpose—the ends justified some unpleasant means. Suddenly, I didn't understand what we were doing here, and I wanted to rip the cold sheet off, cuddle him close to my heart, and run. I wanted to apologize for subjecting him to this pointless, cruel exercise. And it truly felt pointless. It's one thing to hold him down for a lab draw when his blood sugar is cratering. It's another thing to hold him still to be wrapped and dunked in frigid water to satisfy magical thinking. The few remaining scraps of faith I had clung to evaporated like phantoms exposed to daylight. Logic swamped me, screaming inside my head that this water would not help him one damn bit. I realized with terror that I believed precisely nothing—and believed it with all my heart.

Kim looked me in the eye and spoke calmly and evenly. "We'll do it together. We are going to lower him into the water, but his head won't go under."

She held his body and head, and I took his legs.

My eyes were full of tears and my body was shaking. I barely managed to stop myself from mumbling, "Wait! Wait! No, no, no, no!" and stumbling out the door wrapped in a stolen bath towel with my naked child.

When Oscar's body hit the frigid water, his eyes went wide, his arms and legs all flew straight out, and he made an inhuman yelp.

It looked exactly like the beginning of a seizure.

What, oh, what *on earth have I done?* I was nearly beside myself, even after I could see, a few seconds later, that it had not been a seizure after all.

I will never forgive myself for this act of utter madness.

Strung out, breathless, electrified, I quivered in place, barely upright and holding back tears only because there seemed too much wrongness to bother crying about it. Kim handed Oscar back to the volunteers in the dressing room and walked me a few steps over to the adult bath. Another volunteer asked me to lift my right arm and I could barely comply, because I simply couldn't figure out what she was asking me to do. Despite my ineptitude, the attendants managed to wrap me in my own ice-cold, sodden sheet and remove the blue towel in one deft movement. I stepped into the water, and instantly I wailed aloud in dismay, berating myself.

I can't believe I did this to my child.

Again, Kim instructed me to take a moment to collect myself and say whatever prayers I needed to say. I stood there, dumbly, waiting, pretending to pray. Finally, I managed a nearly inaudible mumble: "God, you know what my intentions are. For all the people who have asked for our prayers."

Kim and the other volunteer stood on opposite sides of the bath, grasping my forearms. We walked in tandem to the end of the bath. Kim said, "I want you to sit down, like you're sitting in a chair. Don't lean; we will take care of everything else. We are going to put you in up to your shoulders, but your head won't go under." The icy water enveloped me, and I disappeared.

Until that point, I had felt like a detached observer, but I have no memory of what happened in the bath itself. In a single blink I was facing the opposite direction, ready to step out, my feet so cold I could no longer feel them. I was no longer anxious. I wasn't anything. I felt empty and tired.

We had come to bathe at Lourdes. It was over.

As I dressed, I noted dully that I wasn't "dry" as advertised. One of the miracles of the baths at Lourdes is supposed to be that you are dry as soon as you come out. Well, I wasn't. *Did that wrong too, I guess*, I observed dispassionately.

Oscar was murmuring behind me on the changing table. I heard whimpering and splashing to my right, from another child, the next one in line, already submerged in the spring's water.

I thought, *Someone else is already in there? But we just went; it's still our turn.*

Pulling my sweater over my head, I knocked down a small statue of Our Lady of Lourdes from the shelf nearby, finding the last remaining way to feel even more like an idiot. I picked up the statue, kissed her without feeling, and stood her on the shelf.

I turned to pick up Oscar—relieved that he was back in my charge—and realized with chagrin that he had been with these strangers all along, while I was having a blackout in the next room. He was not perceptibly different. His body still flopped heavily against my chest. I reached for his pacifier and started to put it in his mouth. A volunteer poured a small cup of Lourdes water from a nearby pitcher and told me to dip his pacifier in before I gave it to him. We had been using Lourdes water to mix all his medicines and formula since arriving the day before, and another drop or two was unlikely to make much difference. I could have told her this, but instead I complied.

Oscar was fine. Not healed, but fine.

I have had many powerful, moving experiences of God's personal presence in my life, but this visit to Lourdes had not been one of them. In fact, I felt like the entire thing had happened without me, as if all the work had been done by the hands of the volunteers that lowered us in and carried us out.

Detached. Spent. Empty.

That's that, I thought. *But what was that? Is that simple dunk what we came all this way and waited all this time for? Why?*

I stepped out of my Gethsemane—*let this cup pass me by*—into a day where my son had not been healed, the cup still in front of me, the cross not taken away. I thought of Jesus in Gethsemane, the Son of God, whispering those words to his Father. I thought of the last words he had whispered to me.

This is your cross, and I am not going to take it away from you. I will be with you, and I will help you, but it is yours to carry.

It wasn't as if Jesus hadn't warned me about the outcome.

10.

RAISE YOU UP

Oscar and I waited with our pod for the rest of the malades to leave the baths.

Leaning against the wall along the edge of the river gave me the best view of my fellow pilgrims as they stepped out from the dim, covered courtyard. Some were elated, lit up with divine radiance. Some were in tears—not hysterical tears, but the quiet ones you shed after an encounter that touches your innermost soul. Some seemed almost embarrassed, smiling shyly, overwhelmed by the crush of hugs from the members of the Order as they stepped back into the regular world, the non-heavenly-encounter side.

No one else looked as blank as I felt. Carole and Ryan tried to engage me in small talk, but I steadfastly refused to participate. Eventually, they took the hint and stopped trying, waiting five steps away and craning their necks as they watched for Todd to emerge. Oscar lay quietly in his stroller, sucking his pacifier. I could barely look at him, couldn't make sense of him lying quietly, sucking, the same as he had been an hour ago, and a week before that, and a month before that. Begging for miracles is an all-or-nothing business, requiring a suspension of disbelief that had just been shattered with devastating totality.

We waited a surprisingly long time for Todd to emerge. Had we somehow missed him? Had he left without us, disoriented by glory or overcome with grief? When he finally came out, one of the last pilgrims to finish, I hugged him tightly. We were both quiet. He came over to the stroller and leaned down to give Oscar a kiss. The yawning gap that had stood between us all year seemed as wide as ever. Neither of us had the words, or the wherewithal, to convey our feelings to each other. We stood, surrounding Oscar, together, alone.

After our entire group was finished at the baths, we processed across the bridge to Mass. Ryan was talking lightly on the way out, as he had on the way in, of everything and of nothing.

Directly across the river from the baths stood many sets of candleholders. The tall, rectangular boxes were shielded from the wind on three sides and open to the front. Inside each box, rows of metal holes waited to receive the candles available for purchase at nearby kiosks. The stark black backs of the boxes were decorated with tiny cut-out crosses and the phrase "This flame continues my prayer" in a half-dozen languages. "Questa fiamma prolunga la mia preghiera." "Cette lumière prolonge ma prière." "Das Licht dieser Kerze ist Zeichen meines Betens." The candles stood at jaunty angles, of varying widths and lengths, but all the same snowy white—flames wind-tossed, exploding in brightness, then barely clinging to life. The air was thick with the scent of charred wicks and melted wax that dripped in rivulets over the bars to the floor of the box, the only remaining evidence of worn-out prayers, like desperate words falling from desperate lips until nothing was left to beg for.

I felt myself faltering under the weight of the world's amassed sorrows. Each single candle had been lit by the hand of some unknown individual for an intention dear to that person's heart. I was reminded of our very first procession to Mass, the endless sea of blue voitures, and the certain knowledge that each one carried a suffering too heavy to contemplate. So many prayers cast to the heavens, with only these half-spent candles left to carry them along.

How could the world hold so much pain and not just disintegrate?

How could a human—*one* human, Jesus on the Cross—accept all the suffering of the entire world, past, present, and future?

That idea, which had never particularly troubled me before as a theory, became an impossible horror in the face of these candles. The sorrow they conveyed was beyond the scope of comprehension. Trying to extrapolate from these candles to determine the full expanse of humanity's suffering was like imagining the scale of the entire universe based on the few pinpricks of starlight visible in the night sky.

Ryan stepped to the kiosk, bought one of the largest candles, lit it, and placed it in a holder. He prayed aloud, "Father, we thank you for Oscar and for whatever you have in store for him. Thank you for bringing him to this holy place and allowing our team to care for him. We know the Blessed Mother holds this whole family in her arms today. Bless them, Lord."

Ryan ordinarily had a loud, piercing voice, but here he spoke tenderly, reverently, and his soft hush steadied me. He was maybe not the most reliable charioteer the Order of Malta has ever known, but he *could* call the presence of the Holy Spirit down on cue. He had a remarkable gift for intercessory prayer. Each time he opened his mouth in prayer over us, I felt peace where there had been a storm of angst before.

Because I had entered the baths with Oscar, I turned to Todd as I unbuckled the baby from his stroller. "You should sit with him for this. He and I got to have one special moment already. This one is yours."

Todd protested a bit at first, but he was also moved and eager: "Thanks. I'd like that a lot. Thank you." I nursed a tendency to claim Oscar as my personal possession, to refuse to entrust him to others. Todd is an affectionate and attentive father, but out of nearly three weeks' worth of nights in the hospital, I had spent only one apart from Oscar, under duress. Handing him over to Todd after the baths was an attempt at appeasement that felt like a small death.

The Church of St. Bernadette can be split into multiple worship spaces, and this time we entered the chapel opposite the one where our morning reflection had taken place. The walls of this new space were a bland, washed-out yellow; coupled with the fluorescent lighting, everyone's complexion took on a ghastly, jaundiced pallor. This chapel reminded me of many of the parishes I had attended growing up in the 1980s, where the scratchy upholstered pews and unbroken severity of design had drawn me away from Catholicism in the first place. There had been nothing compelling or sustaining in the practice—or the surroundings—of the faith of my youth. How could I take seriously their belief in the real presence of Christ in the Eucharist, while viewing the ugly austerity of the sanctuaries they had consecrated as a place for Christ to dwell? I'm not sure why I was feeling that same resistance, many years later and half a world away; I suppose I had come to Lourdes imagining I'd encounter more old-world splendor, less modernist brutalism.

Soon we were all gathered in, and I turned my attention to the other pilgrims. I knew the names of many other malades now. Todd was next to Donna, Hugh's wife. Next to her was Laura, a malade whose condition had worsened since our arrival, but who was smiling contentedly now. Not far down the row sat Thomas, a young teenager with congenital limb differences, his father, Steve, standing at his elbow. Elizabeth, a mother from Nebraska, sat with not one but two dark-haired children near the center, pale but shining.

Something about the baths seemed to have tied the pilgrims all together. Even I, with my disoriented and weakened heart, felt the pull of this invisible thread. In the moments before Mass began, there was an excited hum of muffled conversation, where before there had been awkward bursts of small talk. I allowed myself to sink, only a little, into the energy, like hesitatingly dipping a toe into a pool to test the temperature. Everywhere, heads bowed toward each other, as malades recounted what had happened to them in the bath. Laughter and smiling replaced the heaviness of the prayers we had brought with us.

I watched Todd talking animatedly to a man who was seated in his own wheelchair instead of a voiture. Todd threw his head back and laughed, long and loud, at something the man said to him. I hadn't seen him laugh like that in months.

Emboldened, I turned to my neighbor and introduced myself. "Hi, I'm Christy."

"Oscar's mom, right?" She smiled. "Nancy. I'm here with my husband."

"Yes, Oscar's mom," I chuckled. "I might as well just start introducing myself that way. How was your time in the baths?"

She grew solemn, but also somehow joyful, nearly radiating. "It was wonderful, just wonderful. How was yours?"

"It was good. Not what I expected, I guess." I failed to radiate. I kicked myself for asking, for not realizing in advance that the question would be reciprocated. I wasn't prepared to talk about our baths yet, so I redirected the conversation. "Oh, you know what? I have a couple of extra kneepads someone gave me for kneeling on the concrete. Would you like one?"

"Yes, thanks!"

I handed one to Nancy. A gravelly voice behind me broke in: "You don't have one for your friend back here?"

I turned, embarrassed and ready to apologize, but was met with the steady, wry grin of a consummate joker. I tiptoed further into the lighthearted ethos, further from my own brooding. "Nope, sorry, ladies first," I shot back.

We both let out a full-throated laugh. It felt good.

As the opening hymn began, I gave myself over to singing fully, feeling my chest rising and falling, my throat constricting and opening. My body began to ground itself in the physical world again, the world of laughter and breath and chests and throats and song.

After the opening prayer and the readings, the clergy began circulating for the sacrament of Anointing of the Sick.

Catholics believe that each of the seven sacraments is an outward sign of God's grace in the soul. In every sacrament, tangible, earthly items—water, oil, candles—symbolize the life of grace within us. Many sacraments can only be received once, such as Baptism and Holy Orders (ordination to the clergy). Other sacraments, such as Communion and Confession, can be received many times during one lifetime.

Anointing of the Sick is another that can be received repeatedly. Whereas Baptism's graces wash away original sin and welcome us into the family of Christ, the special graces associated with the Anointing of the Sick unite our sufferings with Christ's passion on the Cross. Anointing offers strengthening, forgiveness of sins, and spiritual— sometimes even physical—healing.

I appreciated the dramatic gestures by which we pilgrims had been prepared for this moment. At first, I had been overwhelmed at the thought of the bath and anointing happening on day one, but it made a certain kind of sense now. We were all off-balance and out of our element, so our natural defense mechanisms had been neatly subverted. In that wobbly physical and mental state, we were brought first to Confession and then to the baths. Confession is the sacrament of emptying and surrender, pouring out all the brackish heartache and sin within us; the baths built upon that, inviting us to leave our prayers, worries, and hang-ups at the bottom of the pool, at the feet of Our Lady. If ever in my life I had been an empty receptacle to receive God's grace and let it heal my soul, it was at that moment.

Cardinal Timothy Dolan of New York worked his way down the first row, moving steadily onward toward Todd and Oscar. I left my seat and went to stand with my family, resting my hand on Todd's shoulder, planting a kiss on his cheek. He reached across his chest to take my hand in his, squeezing it. Unlike the bath, where we had been so isolated, we stood now as one unit, one interconnected element of the larger body of supplicants.

Several bishops and cardinals were circulating throughout the malades, and more priests lined the back to anoint the members of the Order. I studied these ordained men, these spiritual giants, bending low, clasping and oiling the hands of the sick, whispering prayers into the ears of the pilgrims and of God.

As I watched Elizabeth between her two children, I could hardly breathe, because the force of her desire for their healing was nearly a visible presence around her. With expectation and trust, the children stretched out their hands, serenely, soberly. On every spot where an anointing was taking place, a spaciousness, an endlessness, seemed to take hold and abide there. *Kairos*, God's time, the eternal now, reached down and overtook *chronos*, our ticking-clock time, even while lines continued to move in a quiet and orderly fashion.

Then Cardinal Dolan was before us. Oscar slumped passively, Todd's hands doing all the work to support him in a seated position. As the cardinal caressed him, Oscar's head lolled backward, his pacifier dangling precariously near the edge of his lips. We rested in silence a moment, while the susurration of continuous prayers swirled around us. Finally, the cardinal dipped his thumb into the Oil of the Infirm and traced a cross on Oscar's forehead, reciting, "Through this holy anointing, may the Lord in his love and mercy help you with the grace of the Holy Spirit."

At these words, Oscar extended his left hand and began to run it slowly up and down through the folds of the prelate's white robe. The cardinal reached down and lightly took that hand, and then Oscar's other one. He traced a cross on each, delivering them with the words "May the Lord who frees you from sin save you and raise you up."

Oscar opened his eyes fully and stared at Cardinal Dolan's face as he spoke.

The blessing was over almost before it began. No jollities or laughter, no personal words of encouragement. Cardinal Dolan moved to the next voiture, where Hugh stood behind his wife, Donna, whose green knit hat hid her thin brown hair. He repeated the exact same gestures, the exact same words. Though I was standing outside that numinous circle where heaven was touching earth and *kairos* supplanting *chronos*, I was an intimate part of Hugh and Donna's prayer. And then Laura's after them. And the next, and the next. Part of the power of the sacraments is in their orderliness and repetition. Because they are impersonal, they transcend the person.

I returned to my seat, and my eyes settled upon the malade directly in front of me, a teenager accompanied by his mother. Her shoulder-length hair curled at the tips; her tanned and weathered face and gray eyes conveyed both toughness and softness. The softness was most evident as she spoke to her son, who was always rocking, sometimes flapping his hands and moaning. As he rocked, he hummed and pressed his fingers to his ears with such force that his knuckles caved in backward; all the while, his mother patted his arm, pulled him gently to his seat each time he began to rise, and murmured soothing words too quiet to hear.

The clergy worked their way around the room. As they approached the boy, he grew more agitated, rocking harder, humming louder. The mother began patting and soothing anew, as perfectly attentive to him as a cloistered nun to chanted prayer. After a few more stops, Cardinal Dolan reached the boy and stretched out his hand. The boy, who had progressed from humming to squealing excitedly, let out a yelp and leaped with the most transparent, unbridled, profound joy I had ever seen. He instantly electrified the room, especially our corner of it.

An elderly Knight behind me stage-whispered to the person next to him, in a Boston accent as thick as clam chowder: "Did you *see* that? Did you see that kid? Wow, that was some excitement. That was *amazing*. Amazing! Did you see the way he jumped up? Boy, that just made my whole afternoon."

The boy was still shouting, and I found I wanted to laugh—not *at* him, but with a spontaneous bubbling of shocking, foreign-to-me joy. I laughed at his delight and at the Knight's delight in him. By the time the Knight had finished his effusive, cartoonish speech, I was doubled over with the effort of containing my own delight. I leaned over to Nancy beside me, jerking my chin back to indicate the man behind us. "And *that* just made mine."

11.

THE DARK NIGHT OF THE SOUL

The candlelight Rosary procession is one of the most well-known Lourdes traditions. Every evening, thousands of pilgrims descend upon the central plaza of the Domain to pray the Rosary together, carrying candles shrouded by tulip-shaped paper surrounds to block the Pyrenean winds. As we processed from our hotel, streams of voitures poured into the central thoroughfares like tributaries draining into a river. It became difficult to maneuver, and our American Association line was broken again and again by French and Dutch and German malades, haphazardly internationalizing our ragtag group.

Carole, consummate grandmother that she was, had asked to sit with Oscar for this walk. He was fast asleep in her arms, and she was grinning broadly with sheer happiness. At the outset we had considered, once again, lugging the stroller along with the voiture, but buoyed by the connection I had felt during the Anointing of the Sick, I felt strongly about keeping Oscar in the voiture whenever possible, united with the malades' common experience.

A Lourdes pilgrimage is characterized mostly by alternate periods of hurrying and waiting. We stood for the better part of an hour, and malades got out of their voitures to stroll and visit. Many of them made a beeline for Oscar, heedless of his unconsciousness. "He's been so good!" "He reminds me of my grandson." "He's just adorable. I'm so glad he's here; it makes me happy to see him."

I couldn't deny the effect that Oscar's presence had on other pilgrims. As I watched and greeted his parade of visitors, I tried to figure it out. He wasn't a mascot, exactly, though his presence had elements of that: a symbol for mass representation, a rallying point, devastating cuteness. There was something else, though. The people who came to him wanted, universally, to touch him. They wanted to be near him. They beamed when he walked by. They stopped what they were doing to adore him. I shrugged and assumed it was because he was the only baby on our pilgrimage, but that didn't explain the depth of the response I was seeing.

We couldn't tell when the procession began, because the crowd was so enormous. Eventually, though, the voitures far in front of us began to roll, and then we were moving. I had changed seats with Carole in the voiture; Oscar and I were tucked in tight under a red fleece blanket with a white Malta cross at its hem, anonymous again in the sea of black, white, red, and blue. As we started to walk, the singing began. The verses were sung far at the front, almost too quiet for us to hear, but every chorus swelled with the thousands of voices around us: *Ave Maria, gratia plena, dominus tecum. Benedicta tu!* "Hail Mary, full of grace, the Lord is with you. Blessed are you!"

The procession began as the sun was setting behind the Rosary Basilica, and at first the light from the candles was hardly visible. As the dusk gathered and clouds descended, their glow shone forth more abundantly, gently illuminating each pilgrim's face. The lonely candles I had seen earlier in the grotto made sense to me now—here, I could see, were the faces they belonged with. After we turned the corner into the main plaza, I saw the priests carrying a cross and a statue of Our Lady of Lourdes at the head of the procession. I turned and could not find the end of it behind me.

We wound our way around the far perimeter of the Domain's grassy plaza before weaving back to fill in the space between the two long arms of the Rosary Basilica. The lines undulated back and forth, winding sinuously, as they slowly edged forward and settled into static rows. The effect was hypnotic, points of light passing each other in the night, left and right and back again. *The light shines in the darkness, and the darkness has not overcome it.* I recited John 1:5 to myself almost reflexively, a biblical salve. The singing continued until every pilgrim was in place, the chorus rising over and over and over again. *Ave Maria, gratia plena*!

When the prayers of the Rosary began, I listened first in confusion, then in awe: every two or three Hail Marys switched to a new language: French. Italian. English. Portuguese. German. Spanish. These I recognized. But some I could not place. Every time a new language was prayed, I could hear a group of voices somewhere nearby in the crowd suddenly gain volume and energy, as they prayed along fervently in their native tongue instead of whispering their prayers over a foreign language. The entire crowd hung together, marking progress with every universal "Amen," whispering along on their own until their language came around again.

By the fourth decade of the Rosary, the wind had picked up and the temperature had dropped twenty degrees. The night had been threatening rain, and it looked increasingly likely. Oscar was awake in my arms now, but quiet. Ryan, playing the responsible charioteer, was concerned. "Should we head back early?"

Todd and I looked at each other. We were soothed, comforted, content, lifted. We were with our people, our suffering universal Church. I think, too, that we were afraid of missing a single thing about this week. Todd lifted an eyebrow (we call this "The Wilkens Eyebrow") and said one word: "Surrender?"

I nodded. We were here to trust that God would take perfect care of us. For the first time in a year, I was feeling as if I *could* trust that. We would stay.

As soon as the last words of the Rosary were uttered, Ryan yanked our voiture out of its row and rushed back to the hotel. We realized it was faster to walk, so I got out of the voiture and handed Oscar to Todd as we hurried through the twists and turns we knew by heart now. The wind whipped sharply down the street, pouring down the tunnel between the high hotels in a rushing torrent, and Todd clutched Oscar like a football, zipped beneath his own sweater. The rain held off until we were a block away; we sprinted into the lobby as heavier drops began to fall.

In our room, I began to undress Oscar, then froze. Todd was talking happily about heading to a bar across the street, where many pilgrims were gathering for a nightcap. I leaned down, then shushed Todd. I listened hard, watching Oscar's chest rise and fall. Observing his neck muscles retract as he fought for air. Hearing a rattle in his chest.

He was wheezing badly.

Todd fetched Kim, who fetched Nurse Selma, the nurse who had appeared as if summoned from a genie bottle during Oscar's seizure at the airport. She brought a doctor with her, a pediatrician we hadn't met yet. Dr. Raggsdorf pulled out a stethoscope and examined Oscar.

"Yes, he sounds wheezy, but I don't hear any crackling. It's not pneumonia, just a bad cold. Do you have a nebulizer?" We did not. "Okay, we'll find you one. I'd also like to start him on some steroids to cut down the inflammation."

"He takes budesonide at home," I offered, slipping back into medicalese as easily as putting on a bathrobe.

"I don't have that, but I think I have some prednisone with me. I'll go see what I've got." She was back with tablets within five minutes, pulled from her medical stores in the hotel. Whipping out a calculator, she figured out his dose and gave us careful instructions. "Here's my card and my room number. Don't hesitate to call at any time if you think he's getting worse tonight." It was already past eleven o'clock, but she was completely earnest.

Dr. Raggsdorf stayed to observe Oscar for another half hour or so, and we passed the time in idle talk, but I was in mental agony. Why had I taken this child, already sick, into a frigid bath and then a long nighttime walk in cold, damp mountain air? Were we going to end up in a French hospital with another round of pneumonia? And for what?

Nurse Selma returned with a nebulizer, a child-sized mask, and albuterol for breathing treatments, somehow procured in this remote French town at nearly midnight. I went slack with relief and gratitude, trying hard to recognize this excellent care as the miracle it was. Once again, Oscar had received better, swifter medical care in this most unlikely of places than he ever did at home.

Once the nurse and doctor had left, though, and Todd had resigned himself to bed instead of the bar, I sat rocking Oscar through his nebulizer treatment and then to sleep. Then I just sat, wide awake, furious with myself and my lack of foresight. Beyond that, I was furious at God. Again. All the peace of the afternoon washed away, and the hellish nightmare of betrayal came roaring back to fill the vacuum.

"We. Are. In. *Lourdes*," I hissed inwardly. "Lourdes, France, home of miraculous cures and spiritual communion. We came all this way to heal him, and fine, I get it, you're not going to do that; you told me already. But you couldn't even heal his cold? You let him get *sicker*? I am trying to do everything you asked of us, God, to surrender to this experience. But the elements of this experience are making him worse. Why are we here? What can I give that I haven't already? *What more do you want from me?*

"And what the hell even was that in the baths? That was weird, and sad, and frankly a little stupid. I don't feel a tiny bit different, even spiritually. That's what we came all this way for?

"Why should I trust you, anyway? You won't even heal a cold!" I cried out in my hubris. I threw myself back on the pillow, pounding the mattress with my fists a few times. I pulled out my Kindle and began to read, my usual bedtime ritual. That night I chose *The Dark Night of the Soul*.

"Spiritual persons suffer great trials," wrote St. John of the Cross, "by reason not so much of the aridities which they suffer, as of the fear which they have of being lost on the road, thinking that all spiritual blessing is over for them and that God has abandoned them since they find no help or pleasure in good things."[1] I read until four in the morning, when I fell into a fitful, dreamless sleep.

12.

Water, Fire, and a Cave

I woke to my iPhone alarm a few short hours later, bleary-eyed and heavy-hearted. *Time to face another day of pointless posturing before an unfeeling God!* My mouth tasted sour, as if I had spent all night holding venom and acid on my tongue. As I checked my phone, I noticed the date. May 6. It had been exactly a year since Oscar's first seizure.

"How did you sleep?" Todd asked.

"I didn't. I stayed awake half the night reading *Dark Night of the Soul* during my dark night of the soul," I muttered back, snappish.

He sighed and rubbed my back. "I was afraid of that."

Walking into the dining room for breakfast, I spotted the mother-son duo who had been sitting in front of me at Mass the day before. The woman waved and invited us to share their table.

"I'm Joyce, and this is Billy," she introduced herself. Her voice sounded exactly like her face looked, roughened and welcoming and warm.

"I sat behind you yesterday," I explained, donning my pulled-together persona like a costume. "It was really beautiful to watch you together. We don't know what to expect yet with Oscar's medical situation in the long run. But seeing you with your son, well . . . it helped. What brought you to Lourdes?" It was far easier to ask questions and listen than to talk.

"It's been a long, hard journey, but Billy is my baby. We go everywhere together." Joyce was uncomfortably direct and forthcoming, with little prompting. "Medically speaking, he should be dead. His doctors told me a few years ago he didn't have much time left, so ever since then, we haven't missed a thing. We go everywhere, do everything we can all the time. And they were wrong. He's still here, better than ever."

"I notice you haven't missed much here in Lourdes, either. I've seen you walking around town," I responded.

"Oh, Billy loves to walk. It's part of his routine. He loves routine. He walks all the time. We walk about four miles a day, wherever we are. They told us he would never walk, but we just kept trying. At first, he could barely stand, then it was one step at a time, but now he loves it and we walk and walk. You'd never know they said he wouldn't walk. Never give up on your kid!" Joyce's sentences tumbled over each other, like happy puppies eager to escape. In the outpouring of words, the desperate depths of her love for him was self-evident. I was usually reticent when it came to Oscar's problems, fearing the listener's boredom or (worse) pity. Joyce shared none of my compunction: Billy was her favorite subject.

She interrupted herself occasionally to speak to Billy. "Here's your spoon, Billy. Use your spoon." Or to pull his hands down when he pressed his fingers to his ears and began to rock. "It's okay, Billy. Do you want some more juice?" Billy seemed oblivious to our presence, keeping up a steady humming underneath Joyce's monologue. I had been hearing his hum in the background for the last two days, without tracing its source. Billy and Joyce moved like extensions of each other's bodies, delicately aligned with invisible wires: she was attuned to his emotional state and he was responsive to her encouragement. I tried to memorize Joyce's words as a balm: "The doctors all say Billy shouldn't even be alive, and look at him. They said he wouldn't walk, and look at him."

As Joyce talked, my brain churned on overdrive, resenting what I perceived as God's lack of responsiveness to our pilgrimage. Billy knew his mother would supply his every need. I felt surer by the hour that God the Father would not supply mine.

Instead of waiting on God's next move, I plotted mine. I wasn't quite bold enough to take this theological question straight to a cardinal, but during our next procession, I jogged ahead to corner our white team chaplain.

"Father, may I speak to you while we walk?"

"Of course. How can I help?"

"I'm Christy, Oscar's mom. I'm having a hard time dealing with my experience in the bath yesterday. Oscar wasn't healed, and okay, I wasn't really expecting him to be, although I do have to admit there was a tiny part of me hoping that maybe God would surprise me. But the whole thing seemed so meaningless. It was a huge letdown. I feel as if I missed something, missed the point, or did something wrong. I couldn't even pray.

"And Oscar had a cold before we came here, and last night it got worse, after the baths—he had to start a bunch of new medications. I should be thankful for the great medical care, and I am; finding a doctor at midnight was a miracle. But I'm mostly angry and confused. I know I should stop fighting for control and just surrender, but I don't know how! I feel like I've turned my whole life over to God and tried to follow his will, but I don't even know what he expects from me anymore. And I don't know what I expect of God. I'm just angry. I'm *so* angry. He can't even cure a cold? What are we doing here?"

Father listened. When he finally did speak, after a thoughtful (agonizing) pause, his voice was tranquil. "That's not how God works. This is all on his time, and you have to let it unfold."

"I know that," I replied. *I know that*, I thought, *but how do you actually* do *that?* "But it's really hard to just . . . do nothing." Listening to myself, I was embarrassed at my childish outburst and wished I could unsay everything.

"You aren't doing nothing. You brought your child here. That took a tremendous act of faith. But this is a different act of faith, what you're being asked now. There's nothing right or wrong about any of this, but you have to trust. The pilgrimage isn't over as soon as the baths are over, or even as soon as you get home. You don't know what God has in store for you, but you can't expect him to reveal his plan on your terms. He called you here for a reason, and you'll know that reason when he decides to show you."

"Okay," I nodded, chastened and thoroughly deflated. My mouth was trying to form the word "but" even though my brain had no idea what could possibly follow it. I stared at the cobblestones, unable to meet Father's eyes, as we walked a few paces in strained silence. "Um, thank you for listening. Will you please pray for me to be able to let go a little?"

"Of course. God be with you."

I trudged back to Todd and Oscar in the voiture and rejoined our pod, walking a step behind the laughing group, tail between my legs.

We processed to Mass at the grotto, the cave where the apparitions occurred. The spring that St. Bernadette dug there still flows today, secured behind a wall of glass in the farthest recess of the grotto. Directly above, the soaring spire of the Basilica of the Immaculate Conception pierces the sky; the church appears to have grown up from roots in the cave itself, a fully formed, Gothic revival stalagmite. The grotto's most famous feature is a towering pyramid of white candles, just off-center, always lit. A statue of the Blessed Mother stands in a niche in the rock, exactly where she appeared to St. Bernadette. Carved at her feet are the words *Que soy era Immaculada Concepciou* (I am the Immaculate Conception).

These words, spoken to St. Bernadette in the local patois by the "beautiful lady" she claimed to have seen, were the linchpin of testimony about the apparitions' validity. Mary never made her name or identity explicit to St. Bernadette, except by this curious moniker. "Immaculate Conception" refers to Mary's own immaculate nature: she was "full of grace" from the first moment of her unborn existence, presaved through Christ's eternal sacrifice on the Cross, a sacrifice that exists in *kairos* and therefore exists simultaneously at every single moment in the *chronos* of human history. It's a complicated theological concept and wasn't a widely understood phrase among the rural French peasantry of 1858. Everyone in Lourdes knew that this poor, ignorant girl could not comprehend what those divine words meant, let alone have dreamed them up to fool the Church authorities. When Mary revealed this name, Bernadette's trustworthiness as a true visionary was sealed.

The morning was bright and cool, but the sun beat down steadily on the stone paving of the unshaded plaza. I perched on a small camp stool next to Todd and Oscar in the voiture. Cardinal Dolan stepped up to the pulpit under the niche, at Our Lady's feet, to preach about three primitive human necessities: water, fire, and a cave. Water is vital to sustain life; it cleans, cools, quenches deep thirsts. Fire provides warmth and protection, has transformative power, and acts as a beacon. A cave has solid, sheltering walls, offering security and comfort.

The sun continued its merciless blaze, and the breeze had died away. We hadn't dressed up Oscar for Mass that morning, leaving him in long-sleeved pajamas so he could nap comfortably. Now he began to squirm and whimper, and the hair around his ears gathered sweat.

"In Lourdes," the cardinal continued, "these three elements carry their age-old meanings, but they carry something else too. The waters of the spring remind us of the waters of our baptism. When we step into the baths, we bring our burdens with us. We leave them there, and something in us dies and is buried in those waters. When we step out, we are fundamentally different in ways we cannot expect."

I shifted uncomfortably and fanned myself with the program. *We are, are we?*

"The flames of these candles represent our petitions. But they also represent the light of Christ at work in our lives. These flames never go out, and neither does the flame of our faith, even when the darkness threatens to overwhelm us."

I wish that were true. Well, I wish I wish it were.

"And inside the walls of this cave, we feel ourselves embraced and protected by the strength and love of the Blessed Mother. We trust that she will shelter us through all storms."

Will she? Will she really?

I could hardly stomach my own audacity. I had fully and freely chosen Catholicism as a well-educated adult. I had clung tenaciously to the outward practice of my faith all through an incredibly dark and challenging year, even when my heart was no longer in it. Now, exactly one year to the day since the whole nightmare had begun, I was sitting inside one of the holiest pilgrimage sites in the world, listening to Mass offered by one of the most beloved and famous cardinals in the world. And I was unmoved. Scoffing, actually.

It was one of the most ludicrous moments of my life.

Anarchy had been loosed upon my family a year ago, my innocence and simple belief drowned. But I knew one thing, only one: I couldn't stay here anymore. It was time to step away from the crossroads. I couldn't hold on to my skepticism and despair along with my faith and hope anymore, without shattering into schizophrenic pieces.

Surrender.

I fought against the sarcastic voice barking inside my brain and tried to accept Cardinal Dolan's words at face value, just a teeny bit. A minuscule act of conscious trust. One deliberate pace down the road that I only wanted to believe (but did not actually believe) was the right one.

Help my unbelief.

By this point, Oscar was sweating profusely and fussing outright. I hopscotched my way to the shade of the rough-hewn stone wall along the side and heaved Oscar's cumbersome body onto my shoulder, bouncing and shushing. He still needed to be comforted like a young infant, although he was three times the size. My arms and head ached, and I wished for some of Joyce's saintly patience. Before long, one of the Dames of Malta stepped over to us.

"He's hot," she said. It felt accusing, though the look on her face was only gentle and concerned. I was so prickly and defensive that everything anyone said to me felt personal, even a homily delivered to twelve hundred pilgrims or a statement of obvious fact.

"I know," I replied with forced politeness. "I brought him over here so we could get out of the sun."

She stepped away and spoke to a nearby child who was carrying a pitcher of water and wearing a red beret. The child handed her a cup of water. From deep inside her voluminous robes, the Dame brought forth a tissue, dampened it in the water, and began to wipe Oscar's brow.

"It's Lourdes water," she explained.

For the rest of the Mass, as I cradled my child, she wiped his forehead with the cool water, moistened the tissue, and wiped again. She never tired and never ceased, even after I began to wish she would leave us alone (well, leave *me* alone—Oscar was mollified). She was utterly absorbed in Oscar and his comfort, lost in her task of service and unmindful of the Mass and everything else around her. After a while, even in my aloofness I was touched by her steadiness. Nothing distracted her from this small, humble act of service.

She worked devotedly until the end of Mass, and then she patted my shoulder and disappeared back into the crowd without a word.

13.

LOWERED THROUGH THE ROOF

Immediately after lunch, Todd and I walked to our assigned reflection group for caregivers who were parents of child malades. Even
among a sea of people intimately familiar with challenging illnesses,
we were a small, intimate breed of our own: Me. Todd. Elizabeth, the
mother of the two young malades. Steve, the father of Thomas, the
boy with limb differences. And Joyce, Billy's mother, our breakfast
companion.

Our chaplain, a monsignor, opened with a short prayer, then read
from the story of the paralytic man whose four friends lowered him
through the roof on a mat when they could not reach Jesus any other
way (Luke 5:17–26). Monsignor read the passage slowly and prayer-
fully, a prelude to our discussion about the gospel, in the style of lectio
divina. As I entered the story in my imagination, key passages leapt
out, as if they were written just for me. Monsignor invited us to share
any thoughts or inspirations we had after the reading.

Why are you thinking these things in your hearts? Jesus chided the
Pharisees who questioned his ability to forgive sins, let alone heal. The
sentence stuck in my throat like a bone. I thought back to my botched,
goofy conversation that morning with our chaplain and recognized
myself in the Pharisees in the story. I kept pigeonholing God, telling
him how he was allowed to work, being affronted when he failed to
obey my every whim. My face burned.

"I always found it interesting," remarked Steve, "that the physical
healing here was almost an afterthought. The spiritual healing came

first; the physical healing Jesus performed out of exasperation more than anything, as a way of calling attention to the spiritual healing that had already happened."

"That was true in many of Jesus' miracles of healing," agreed Monsignor. I had heard this gospel passage countless times, and I had noticed before that Jesus didn't heal the man's paralysis first, but second. But how had I not noticed that this seemed *intentional*—that it indicated an order of importance? The physical healing might have been granted strictly as a way to prove to the Pharisees that Jesus was capable of all the things he said he was. Jesus might have been content to let the man leave with the spiritual healing, but not the physical. I wondered whether the paralyzed man on the mat would have been content with that too.

"Anyone else?" he encouraged.

"Remarkable things," I blurted out. "I wonder about remarkable things. Why do they seem so rare these days? I mean, no one traveling with us, as far as I know, was miraculously healed in the baths yesterday. No instant, total healing." I wondered, but didn't ask aloud, why I seemed to be the only one among our fellow pilgrims who couldn't accept that with dignity. "I guess I'm impatient to get to the end of all these stories, the stories of everyone on this pilgrimage. I want to believe that God has remarkable things in store, but if I'm being honest, I kind of don't. I'm not sure what we're supposed to get out of this trip."

The group was quiet after I finished, shifting restlessly. No one offered any pat answers. I tried to be grateful for that small mercy.

Monsignor opened the floor to more general discussion then, and there was surprisingly little preliminary chitchat; we recognized kindred spirits in each other and agreed, without speaking words to this effect, that it was time to get to work. We took turns introducing ourselves and our families briefly, describing what our pilgrimage had been like so far. In Elizabeth, especially, I felt a connection: we were close in age and both had many young children, with a medically fragile child in the mix. She voiced my own uncertainty and frustration, the complications of a mundane daily existence seasoned liberally with profound physical and spiritual crises. I heard, too, her frail hope, the beginnings of an exhalation far too long in coming.

When it came to our turn, Todd did most of the talking for us both; I would have just been echoing everything Elizabeth said. As he spoke, I was amazed, bewildered, and even a little hurt at his equanimity, as usual. "Oscar is such a blessing to us, and we're really grateful to be here. I can already see how just being taken care of is working on our hearts. It's a relief." He took so much in stride, all the small agonies and worries that I carried around, what felt like the entire world perched precariously and painfully on my shoulders.

When it was Joyce's turn to speak, she took off at a clip, true to form, with little prompting or self-censoring.

"Billy's my youngest of ten." As she continued prattling on, I sat up straighter and looked at her sharply. Ten kids, and she failed to mention that over breakfast?

"I work full-time at a school for troubled youth, but I raised all my kids myself." She recounted this like it was a completely ordinary accomplishment, but I was astounded. She raised ten kids alone, cared for a fully dependent child like Billy, and worked a full-time job caring for still others, while I could barely manage to get myself dressed some days. Rule number one of staying sane as a mother is not to compare yourself to other mothers, but it was difficult not to feel indicted by Joyce's sheer capability.

"A lot of my kids have fallen away from the Church, but I just love Jesus and the Blessed Mother so much. She's been so good to me." Joyce had turned her life over to Christ in ways that looked ridiculous, and by many measures, she had failed. Her kids weren't Catholic. Yet she wasn't wailing in despair or running away or gnashing her teeth or shaking her fist at God.

By this point, I was beginning to squirm, as Joyce's life story shot down my internal excuses for my unhappiness one by one, like ducks in a carnival gallery.

"The hardest time was with one of my other sons. He was killed in a robbery gone wrong a few years ago."

You could have heard a pin drop. Joyce had spoken almost without taking a breath for several minutes. For a while, we had been

nodding along, waiting politely for her to finish and give someone else
a turn as our limited time ticked away. At this last revelation, though,
she had the instant and complete focus of the entire room.

"That was really hard, but I trust in God's mercy. I know he's okay.
I know I'll see him again, and I just ask the Blessed Mother to take
care of him until I get there."

I had spent twelve months wrapped preciously in a manufactured
cocoon of self-pity and bruised feelings. What I was going through
appeared, at least to my eyes, to be a lot worse than what other people
were dealing with. Cancer? Divorce? Dying parents? Run-of-the-mill
burdens—life sucks sometimes. I was sure I had it worse than anyone
I knew. Almost no one else I knew in real life had a permanently,
profoundly disabled child.

Until now.

Joyce did. She saw my disabled child and raised me four extra kids
above and beyond my brood of six, plus a full-time job caring for the
elderly, children fallen away from faith, and violent crime. With her
unvarnished testimony, Joyce had unwittingly thrown a lit match at
my cocoon and burned it away instantaneously. I felt both naked and
ashamed and awed and inspired at the same time—which was not at
all healing or pleasant, just an exposure of my self-pity for what it was:
lies, a crutch, a barricade.

I did not, it turned out, have a lock on the worst suffering in the
world—or even in this very small room.

When it was Steve's turn to speak, the conversation took an opposite turn. "I'm a youth minister for our diocese, so I live and breathe
theology all day long," he explained. "I truly understand the idea of
redemptive suffering. But I feel really abandoned by our community.
We get a lot of pity and concern, but not much actual help, you know?
Raising a kid with disabilities is complicated and isolating, and sometimes just prayers and good thoughts aren't enough. We just figure out
how to do it on our own, because we don't have a choice."

He continued speaking, growing agitated to the point of tears.
How trapped they felt. How little material support they had, with no
family nearby and no ability to move due to the specialized nature
of his job.

Joyce's testimony had shown me the futility and selfishness of my self-pity, but Steve's had a markedly different effect. I heard anger in his cracking voice, saw it in the set of his jawline. And oh, did I recognize that anger. Anger and I were old friends. But never before had I heard it in someone else's voice, seen it staring out of another person's eyes. As Steve spoke words I knew I had spoken before, describing a situation that could have been mine, his anger was profoundly disturbing. I recoiled from it, instinctively. I knew, *knew*, quite suddenly and to the tips of my toes, that this anger was not from God.

Steve's anger was twisting him from the inside out, and God was not behind that, but I was pretty sure I knew who was.

Joyce had acted as a sort of Ghost of Christmas Past for me, generating an alternate reality almost fully formed in my mind, one in which I had lived the last twelve months without constantly laboring under the oppression of anxiety and despair, but instead with grace and trust. Steve, wrestling openly with his literal inner demons, was my Ghost of Christmas Present. The hurt, the confusion, the anger—all of it was mine.

I leaned in, expectant and tense, as Monsignor met Steve where he was, gently. Everyone on the pilgrimage with us was so, so impossibly gentle. His words were for me, too, although neither of them knew it.

"But we have to rely on community," explained the chaplain. "We must make ourselves vulnerable to others in order to be healed. The paralytic in our story was only saved by the faith of his friends. The community bore him forth to Christ, and it was *their* faith that moved Jesus to act, not the man's. He couldn't have gotten there on his own. We don't even know if he wanted to go. Maybe he was angry and yelling at them to stop the whole time. Maybe he didn't believe Jesus could heal him."

Monsignor paused to let that soak in, then pressed us one step further. "Was he even ready or willing to accept his miracle?"

14.

Outward Signs, Inward Grace

When we wrapped up our discussion, we barely had time to run back and retrieve Oscar, pack up food and gear, and get lined up for the next procession: a eucharistic procession, adoration, and benediction in the Rosary Basilica plaza.

In a eucharistic procession, the Body of Christ is carried in a monstrance high at the front of a procession of clergy, followed by worshipers. Hymns are sung and prayers are recited until everyone is in place, and then the entire assembly spends an hour together in prayer in front of the Blessed Sacrament.

As we lined up, Todd leaned over and said, "More than one person told me that of all the healing miracles that occur at Lourdes, most of them occur during the eucharistic procession, not in the baths."

Okay, God. Last chance to knock my socks off.

The day could not have been more triumphantly beautiful. Every pretravel communication we received strongly suggested we pack for cold, rainy weather. But it was in the seventies and sunny the entire week, except for the brief cold shower after the previous night's Rosary. Saturday afternoon was mild and glorious. The blaze of the sun was tempered now by a few clouds and a freshening breeze off the mountains.

Oscar sat with his back against my chest, pacifier in place. As we walked, he sat up straighter, then he reached across my lap to grab the side of our voiture with both hands. He began to pull himself up, and I helped him to his knees. He held on to his pose and his pacifier, watching the other processing pilgrims with interest. This first spark of liveliness I had seen in him since our arrival warmed my heart. I kissed the top of his downy head, grateful that his new cold medicine was working. He was feeling better, waking up to the wonder around him.

We continued our slow, stately walk, passing through the dissipating clouds of incense trailing behind the monstrance. Music emanated from every corner of the Domain, and I looked around to find its source. Carole elbowed me and nodded upward with her chin, chuckling with a wry grin, "In Lourdes, even the trees sing." I smiled when I realized what she meant: speakers were hidden in the trees and under the buttresses of the cathedral, pouring out music. Lourdes reminded me of Disney World, another place where the entire sensory experience is carefully orchestrated to evoke an emotional response—there happiness, here peace.

All the pilgrims could join in every hymn refrain since they were simple melodies with few words, easily learned. The chants were repeated endlessly like tolling bells, rising along with the incense from every corner into the blue heavens.

After about thirty minutes of slow walking and prayerful singing, the plaza was packed with pilgrims, front to back and side to side; more lined the walkways around every side and the bridge across the top. Our group ended up at the back. The clergy, robed in white and packed across the entire front steps of the Rosary Basilica, were so far from us that they looked like tiny figurines gliding about on the raised steps under the arches.

Todd dropped to his knees alongside the voiture and pulled out his rosary. Oscar was transfixed by all the commotion, the sensory swirl of colors and noise and light. As much as I wanted to kneel, too, I was enjoying watching Oscar. He was alert, content. For almost a half hour, he had alternated between pulling himself to a kneel and sitting back down on my lap, with a strength and purpose I hadn't yet seen on our trip. He was acting more like himself, his very best self, the self we occasionally saw at home in between episodes of seizures and sleep deprivation. The people most capable of coaxing this level of sustained interest out of him were his cadre of highly trained therapists and his grandpa (my dad, inarguably Oscar's favorite person in the world).

No one was coaxing or cajoling here. Oscar watched with interest, squirming in my lap to get a better view of the goings-on. He became so squirmy that I dug out his favorite spinning toy. He held and regarded it for a few moments, shaking it once or twice as if undecided, and then, instead of his usual habit of spinning his favorite rung with pathological focus, he began gleefully banging the hard plastic against the metal sides of the voiture. I unwound his fingers and handed him his rosary instead, a string of bright silicone beads designed for chewing. He happily shoved several into his mouth and cooed, drool running everywhere.

The sky shimmered, the birds twittered in the trees, the air was festooned with scent and song. I alternated between praying and studying the people around me. The dynamic of our group, and of the entire assemblage, seemed markedly different from when we first arrived. Earlier, their faces had showcased a wide array of emotions, each stark and obvious: anticipation, fear, nervousness, sorrow. Now, contentment and joy had displaced all these, winding among the wheels of our voitures, knitting us together into a single unit of prayer. Nearly every face was smiling. Everyone who caught my eye smiled, if they hadn't already been smiling. I had never known smiles could have so many shades before, because they had never been arrayed in one place for my comparison. Utter delight. Soft knowing. Excited expectation. Happy longing. Complete trust.

Todd was still kneeling. I thought back to the Friday morning reflection. Had that just been the previous day, that yesterday time that felt so long ago now, before the baths? I remembered how my intrepid, devout husband had knelt the entire time, and how his knees had been studded with impressions of the pebbled concrete for the rest of the day. And I felt again the twinge of jealousy and even annoyance that he was so wrapped up in his individual prayer. How did he keep *doing* that, in this majestic scene full of beautiful and interesting distractions? I tapped him on the shoulder to see if he wanted to trade places and take a seat in the voiture, but he remained motionless, back turned to me, head bowed. I took up my rosary again, shrugging at our voiture-neighbor with a wry grin. (Oh, there's another species of smile.)

A moment, an hour, an eternity later, the priests and a dozen attendants left the steps and processed throughout the crowd bearing the monstrance aloft. Most people crossed themselves or even got down on their knees as the Blessed Sacrament passed by, as the eye of Christ gazed upon them. I squeezed Oscar, bowed my head, and thanked God (sincerely and fully, for a change) for having brought us so far, both in time and in space, from where we had started a year ago.

Todd didn't move. He was so engrossed, he missed the highlight of the service: benediction, a blessing imparted from Christ himself through his presence in the Eucharist, happening not twenty feet in front of us, while my husband knelt, unresponsive, deep in trance-like prayer.

No one, so far as I could see, fell to the ground, speaking in tongues or throwing away crutches. Oscar had dozed off in my lap. The decidedly nonmiraculous procession ended, and we waited our turn to be wheeled out of the plaza, back into the crowded hubbub of the marketplace of Lourdes.

About halfway back along our usual route, we passed the shop of a photographer who had attended the Anointing of the Sick with us the day before. I asked Carole if she wanted to hold Oscar. ("Yes!" she answered immediately. Carole always wanted to hold Oscar.) She hopped in and I hopped out, and Todd and I joined hands, strolling into the tiny shop.

Every wall was lined from top to bottom with proofs of photos from various pilgrimage groups. Many of our fellow travelers were already inside, combing through our group's pictures, which covered a twelve-foot stretch of wall. I studied each briefly as I passed, reading faces again. I was beginning to sense that one of the peculiarities of Lourdes, one of the traits that set it apart from the normal course of everyday existence, was that the entire range of human emotion was on display everywhere you looked. You couldn't walk through the sanctuary without bearing close witness to tenderness, agony, trust, astonishment, fear, grief, ecstasy. You don't see these things in your average coffee shop, or even in an average pew in an average church.

Here they were ordered in staggering arrays, papered to the walls of this incredible studio. The resulting tableau was a masterwork of human psychology. I marveled at the incomprehensible amount of emotional processing that went on in Lourdes, hour after day after year.

But then again, no—not the *entire* range of human emotion. You would be hard-pressed to find hatred in Lourdes, or disgust. Not that they aren't there in the town, as they are in every place that humans dwell. But as far as I had seen, they were absent from the sanctuary itself. It must be complicated to live a regular life in a town like Lourdes. I speculated about the homes of the people behind the shop counters. Who did they fall in love with? Where did they buy groceries? What personal vendettas were they discussing after hours, over bottles of Bordeaux? Were there murders in Lourdes? I had visited and lived in enough interesting places to know the strong divide between tourists and townies, yet here so many of the tourists were not just tourists, but earnest spiritual seekers; every townie, by extension, played a role in that search, for good or ill.

I started tracing my fingers down the lines between the photos, looking for familiar faces. In the top row, I stopped.

Oscar.

The shot was taken from behind Todd, over his shoulder. Oscar was sitting on Todd's lap, facing the camera. The strong, veiny hands I loved so well cradled Oscar's hip and his head, while the baby lounged backward, relaxed and comfortable. His golden downy hair, fine as silk, stuck out in several directions. His eyes were open and keen, fixed on Todd's face. And his mouth was pursed, but slightly open, as if Oscar were interrupted midsentence, or while trying to blow a kiss, whistling a happy tune, or doing any one of a number of mouth-related things he couldn't actually do. In the photo, though, it looked like he could. It looked like he could do anything. The photo had captured Oscar in an unguarded moment, giving the baffling impression that when I wasn't watching my son, he carelessly dropped his pretense of being a nonverbal, disabled child and passed the time having a wise, clear-headed chat with his father.

We had many photos of Oscar at home. In almost all of them, his gaze was unfocused or elsewhere. Many shots also featured various therapeutic equipment or medical supplies. But this could have been just any baby, just hanging out with any dad. Except he was ours. And he *was* nonverbal. He was a malade. This was what illness and disability looked like in him—this peaceful satisfaction that I had seen without seeing it, that I had watched my son live out but not yet believed in.

I tugged at Todd's sleeve. "Look." He followed my finger and wrapped his arm around my waist. I rested my head against his shoulder, and together we admired our beautiful, disabled, ordinary boy.

Someone walked up behind us and said, "Did you see your picture?"

"Yes, this one," I murmured, without turning around. "Isn't it amazing?"

"No, *this* one." Whoever it was grabbed my hand.

I let my arm drag behind and graze along Todd's arm until I reached his hand and clasped his fingers in mine, pulling him along.

"Over here. Third row, near the door." The anonymous hand reached in front of me and pointed, then melted back into the crowd without another word.

Cardinal Dolan held Oscar's pudgy hands in his prodigious ones, as he spoke the words of anointing: *May the Lord who frees you from sin save you and raise you up.* The photo blurred as my eyes filled with gratitude and joy.

I had been struggling all week to understand what was happening to my family, as it was happening. I felt two steps behind or ten paces ahead, only rarely engaging in the thing that was happening in the present, simply and honestly. Todd was always fully focused and enmeshed in every aspect of the experience, spiritually filled by the literal presence of Christ, kneeling for hours without interruption or pain, while my anxious brain refused to turn off.

As I stared at the photo, though, I saw living-color proof of the grace surrounding us, a touchpoint to help me begin to process one step of the journey. Whatever I felt—or did not feel—this was a tangible emblem of one of the many gifts we had already received.

A sacrament of the Church is an outward sign of inward grace. Like the Pharisees questioning the healing of the paralyzed man on his mat, I was disinclined to trust this inward grace. *Who is this fellow who speaks blasphemy? Who can forgive sins but God alone?* The physical signs (the oil, the words) should have served to help, but I was too well practiced in being untrusting, after a full year of walking exclusively in that rut.

Now I was staring at another physical sign, one that even the Pharisees had not enjoyed—photographic proof of the outward sign and inward grace alike. Whatever happened, during or after this pilgrimage, our son had already been chosen and blessed. It took seeing that blessing with my own unbelieving eyes (or maybe it took the distance of being a step removed, seeing it through the lens of a camera) to awaken to the gift that was unfolding for us. The blessings were already happening; some had already happened.

We had come to surrender our son in trust, and here—I could see for myself—my husband had surrendered him willingly to the care of Christ, through the instrumental hands of the cardinal. In the picture I was behind them, smiling peacefully. I closed my eyes and called up the moment in my mind again. That's right. I had felt peaceful as I watched. It was only afterward that my joy had collapsed, as I decried God, as the Pharisees had, for failing to produce the physical healing and protection I demanded as proof.

Steve's comment during our afternoon reflection with the other caregivers rang in my ears. *The physical healing was an afterthought . . . a way of calling attention to the spiritual healing that had already happened.*

15.

Nothing a Bottle
of Wine Can't Solve

Saturday evening, the Knights and Dames of Malta planned activities for the malades at the hotel, and the caregivers were turned loose to enjoy a free evening on the town. No program, no agenda, no medication reminders or medical procedures. My parents back home were extremely capable caregivers for our children, and we were fortunate also to have a stellar regular sitter, so we did manage to enjoy the occasional evening out, but those nights were squeezed into otherwise hectic weeks. Half the time we were so exhausted that we had to fight valiantly just to stay out past our children's bedtimes and make the babysitting time worthwhile.

In Lourdes, we had enjoyed three days of help and companionship, fresh air and sunshine, prayer and meditation, freedom from obligations. Although the demanding schedule was exhausting, we had been refreshed by the change and the company.

Now, all that was about to be topped off with a date night in France!

Carole, veteran of nineteen straight trips to Lourdes, offered a handful of suggestions for good places to dine. We wanted something local and adventurous, not just one of the tourist cafes. Armed with a list of possibilities, we left Oscar fed, medicated, and ready for bed, lovingly attended by his "Auntie" Kim, and set out into the cool of the dusky evening.

Todd and I walked up a hill toward the center of town, away from the sanctuary and the surrounding hotels. The last time Todd and I had wandered arm in arm through a European city together had been sixteen years earlier, before we were married, during the trip when I had pooh-poohed the chance to visit Lourdes with my grandmother's choir. Wandering a European street with no objective other than finding a good meal, I felt grounded, real, present in a way I hadn't since—well, I couldn't remember when.

Then we got to the cafe, and it was closed.

We looked at each other and burst out laughing. I had conveniently forgotten the part of travel that involves miscalculation and redirection. "Okay, what's next on the list?" I asked.

We were free with each other, easy and relaxed, playacting at openness, but with reasonable success for a change. We had publicly referred to ourselves as "Team Wilkens" ever since we had been a team of just two, not eight—our oldest child even received a custom "Team Wilkens" onesie before she was born, worn by each of our children over the ensuing decade. But for a long time, we hadn't been a team. We coexisted and inhabited the same general spaces, but the synergy was missing. As I took my husband's hand that night, a current passed between us, a warmth and connection reminiscent of the long-ago days when flirtation had been like oxygen, urging on the first kindling of our affection. "Hey," I tugged his hand and stopped.

He looked at me, Wilkens eyebrow arched. "Hey."

I wrapped myself tightly around his shoulders and kissed him full on the lips in the middle of a side-alley street in a medieval French village. "I love you."

Todd's smile started at one corner of his mouth, like it always did, but it didn't stop there this time, as it did so often those days. It spread to encompass his whole face, his eyes, then even down to his shoulders and arms, which released their tension.

He kissed me back. "I love you too."

As we trekked back down the hill, we searched for easy conversation, settling on gossip about the members of our pod. "Poor Ryan," I laughed. "He really is trying, but I still don't think he's out of the doghouse with Kim."

"No, he's not," Todd agreed. "At least he's got a good sense of humor about himself."

"He's such an interesting character. Everyone is. I'm amazed at every single person I've met," I continued. "I feel a bit like God chose us all for each other. Don't you? Like he brought these exact people together at this exact time and place?"

"I know what you mean. And some of the members have done this every year for twenty or thirty years. Kim says it's like this every time," he answered.

I nodded. "She calls it *sacred synchronicity*—she's said that more than once. I keep wondering what God is going to do with all these connections."

"Me too." He squeezed my hand, and we walked in silence for a while.

We walked along the main tourist drag and stopped at a place we had passed a dozen times. No intimate sidewalk cafe or gourmet high-end restaurant, this one had a giant menu on the outside wall, with prices prominently displayed.

I turned to Todd. He shrugged and smiled, just the corner-of-the-mouth smile this time. "Whatever you want," he agreed amiably.

"It doesn't really matter. It's a date wherever we go," I encouraged.

He stepped forward. "Let's see how long the wait is."

We were seated right away, with that charming European custom of squeezing customers into any available seat. Our table was on the back terrace, overlooking the Gave River. Around us was a veritable Babel of languages; nearly everyone was either wearing the uniform or the name tag of an Order of Malta pilgrimage. As we waited an interminably long time to place our order, we chatted with the British ladies at the table next to us. They enthusiastically recommended their entrees, the bread, the bottle of wine that explained their loquacious mood.

As the wait continued, Todd and I tried to decipher what we could of the menu. "I want something classic French," he announced.

I pointed to one of the local specials. "How about this? Some kind of duck stew. And I really want liver. I never get to eat liver because you all hate it so much. I'll have . . . hmm, *fois frais*. Cold liver? Is that right?" My college French was decidedly rusty. "Well, sounds weird, but that's what I'm going to try."

At last, our harried waiter frantically cleared the table next to us, which the women had vacated ten minutes ago. He knocked over the bread and water on the table in his haste, apologizing, "It's very busy tonight." Todd and I were in such easygoing moods, charmed by the walk and the river's babbling, that we found the bread-toppling hilarious. Our wine arrived shortly, and as we sipped, we took in the infectious energy of the boisterous crowd around us. Between the energy, the wine, the freedom, and our empty stomachs, our laughter loosened even more.

Todd looked at something over my shoulder and pointed with his chin. "Check out that guy's power wheelchair. It's like a monster truck. Monster chair."

I twisted in my seat to look. At the booth directly behind me, a rotund, elderly Knight of Malta with the emblem of Britain on his shoulder sat on a wheelchair seat fully three feet off the ground, like a power-chair throne. Its base was the size of our entire tabletop. As I watched, he was trying to maneuver his chair into position, very badly. He misaimed and pushed two tables askew. He turned around to back into a better spot, but motored into the back of the booth behind him, and then kept going, until the booth tipped forward several inches. He powered forward again, and the glasses wobbled on the table next to him. He was perfectly oblivious to the trail of destruction in his wake, face composed and inscrutable.

"Whoa. That is intense." I turned back around and tried to give Todd a this-is-serious look, but we both burst out laughing. I loved this British Knight's bravado. I loved this Texan man's laugh.

When our dinner arrived, we alternated between exclamations of pleasure and appreciative, mindful chewing. In France, even the sidewalk tourist cafes produce delicious meals. Todd's duck, fatty and falling off the bone, came in a bowl with tender vegetables, all submerged in a decadent gravy. My "cold liver" turned out to be fried liver and another example in support of Todd's life axiom that anything good to eat can only be improved by frying it. We tasted and traded and sipped, sopping every bit of the savory brown sauces with the crusty bread, smearing butter on anything that wasn't nailed down.

We had talked cheerfully but gingerly all night, in fits and bursts, like college students on a blind date. Any substantial, difficult topic was studiously avoided. The cadence of our conversation was lopsided: entire extemporaneous speeches or brief asides, punctuated by extended silences. Our eyes would meet accidentally, then rove clumsily around the room, and we fell back on the niceties of table manners too often. ("More wine?") But we were trying. We were both trying so hard.

The camaraderie inside the restaurant, inside the whole town, gave rise to a thought, and a half bottle of wine helped it come spilling out whole. "I feel like this is what people mean when they say heaven on earth," I blurted out. "The whole town is full of all this suffering, enormous suffering, but it's not hard. Everyone who needs help is helped. They're not treated like a burden." I paused for a beat. "I feel like this is what the whole world is supposed to be. Could be."

Todd leaned back in his chair, sipping his wine thoughtfully. He didn't answer, just nodded and looked at me.

"This is what it means to say we are all members of the Body of Christ. I mean, I understood that in a theoretical way before, but this is what it actually looks like. These people are literally Christ's hands and feet to us, and all of the things that have been so hard all year, *so* hard, aren't hard anymore. Not here. They take such delight in Oscar. Not pity, just delight."

It was the only serious turn the conversation took that night. We were still so fragile, so weary of difficulty—the difficulty of our lives, but also the difficulty of talking about Real Things without stepping on a conversational landmine. I didn't have any idea what was going on in my husband's head, or how he was processing any of the pilgrimage. Neither of us was quite ready to talk out what was happening to us in this place, not even Todd, though he usually can't think through any complicated input without verbalizing it.

This had been a sticking point for our entire relationship. Me, Christy the introvert, ruminating entirely in my head, dumping out an entire emotional load at once like a finished sculpture, then scurrying back to my cave as the dust settled. I need time to think in between volleys. Todd the extrovert, talking around every possible angle, building arguments on the fly, trying and failing to engage his frazzled wife and her overwhelmed brain with all the words at once. He hated leaving a conversation unfinished. I was always the one who broke first, shutting down just when things picked up steam and really needed (from Todd's point of view) to be resolved.

We had spent most of the year just not talking. Under tremendous stress, the pattern of our worst marital behaviors had become amplified. But that night, we began to talk, carefully. Not about Oscar or our hopes, prayers, and fears, but about the people we had met that week. Our five other kids. The wine. The glorious weather. It felt like a reunion after months of separation.

As we left the restaurant to head back to the hotel, we ran into Ryan with a group of friends, who were heading out for their own night on the town. "Going back already? You should go get a drink!" he told us. "Oscar is *out*. The doctor and the nurse have both been by to check on him, and they said he was great. Go enjoy your freedom!"

We didn't need to be told twice. Even another minute of this second-spring romance was welcome. We clasped hands again and headed across the river to the Hotel Jeanne d'Arc, where Todd had planned to go the night before until we noticed Oscar's wheezing. As we crossed, a very rowdy karaoke rendition of "Piano Man" poured out onto the street. We stepped inside and melted together into the raucous wall of sound, in the mood for a melody.

16.

The Beloved

"If you thought the candlelight Rosary procession was something, just wait," Kim proclaimed as we lined up for Sunday morning's procession. "The International Mass is quite a spectacle."

During the first weekend of May, every Order of Malta association in the world sends a delegation to Lourdes. Something like ten thousand pilgrims—malades, their caregivers, doctors, nurses, clergy, Knights, Dames, auxiliary members, and volunteers—descend upon the tiny village in that single weekend.

Over the course of our days in France, the streets had become increasingly crowded with pilgrims in various national Malta uniforms. Every European country was amply represented, as well as many nations from farther afield: Lebanon, Australia, South Korea, even Syria. Our hotels were quiet and isolated at the far edge of town, but each time we processed to the Domain, more pedestrians and voitures cut through the middle of our line, and the streets became more choked with black-and-red uniforms.

On Thursday, we had enjoyed a straight and uninterrupted shot to the Rosary Basilica for the opening Mass; on Saturday, our walk to the same spot for the eucharistic procession had taken three times as long. For this day's International Mass, every single pilgrim from every nation who had traveled with a Malta association to Lourdes would be in the same place at the same time, crowded into the Basilica of St. Pius X, a basilica built underground to prepare for the 1958 centennial celebration of the Lourdes apparitions.

We chatted with the other malades and pod teams around us, especially Megan and Chase, who always lined up behind us. The young couple had come to give thanks for Megan's healing from advanced colon cancer—in her early twenties, just after the birth of their first child. She had toted her newborn infant along to every radiation treatment for six weeks. (Here's one thing about Lourdes: it is impossible to feel sorry for yourself for very long, because someone always has a worse story than you. Always.) The bonds among the pilgrims were strengthening each day, reminding me of the friendships I'd formed during various summer camps as a child: quick but startlingly deep, built on intense shared experience. I was still in touch with a couple of those summer-camp friends, twenty-five years later, and I knew instinctively that the same would be true of many fellow travelers here.

I felt especially close to the members of our pod. Kim and Carole functioned as surrogate grandmothers to Oscar, right down to arguing good-naturedly over whose turn it was to hold him or babysit during a nap. Amy was more reserved, as am I, but I enjoyed getting to experience the novelty of the week with another first-time pilgrim (and fellow introvert). Ryan—affable, funny, kind—had spent the week providing a lighthearted note we all badly needed.

I knew the underground basilica was under the grassy plain at the end of the Domain, but I hadn't seen an entrance anywhere. As we walked along the plaza, our procession line made a sharp turn behind a concrete wall, and I found myself staring into an enormous tunnel, long, wide, and tall, the kind you might see leading into the bleachers at a football stadium. Instead of up into bright sunshine, this one curved down and away into mysterious darkness.

With every continued step, I felt more and more like we were descending into a concrete bunker. The procession lines flowed in like molasses as the line bottlenecked; we were being packed in like sardines. My imagination leapt to visions of early Christians herded into the Coliseum and the fragile remnants of modern religious communities pushed into hiding. I uttered a whispered prayer for persecuted believers everywhere, fantasizing for a terrible split second that my fellow pilgrims and I were all that remained of Christianity in the entire world.

We reached the end of the tunnel and entered the basilica. Immediately to our right, the priests who would concelebrate Mass were congregating. To put that in perspective, remember that every Malta association in the world sent a delegation to Lourdes that weekend. In that corner, every deacon, priest, bishop, archbishop, and cardinal that had traveled with any of them was standing idly in his Easter-season vestments. Several hundred clergy members milled around, waiting for Mass to start. *All that remains of Christianity in the entire world,* I thought to myself.

The cavernous indoor space was supported by angular concrete struts. I tried to take in its entirety—embracing and sturdy, ugly but comforting, like someone's favorite old sweater or Grandma's lived-in basement. Giant concrete ribs lined the ceiling from one end to the other, covering an area that could easily contain a football field. Around the perimeter hung massive banners, each bearing the image and name of a saint, their scale and number so huge that I couldn't hope to see them all from where I was standing. The banners, reminiscent of retired sports jerseys, reinforced the stadium feel, as did the extravagant and unrestrained use of concrete.

Kim, concerned yet again that we would be stuck with Oscar's stroller in the middle of a long, immovable line of voitures, took matters into her own hands and marched us up the long aisle toward the altar in the very center of the basilica. She was intercepted by a hospitaller, who deposited us in the second row. "I'll meet you at the St. Michael's Gate after Mass," Kim instructed us. "The nearest exit is over there." She pointed to an exit sign unreachable behind six hundred people. She hugged us goodbye, and we were left to ourselves, together, alone, surrounded.

We were only about twenty feet from the raised altar. I couldn't believe our luck, especially after I turned around. The sea of bodies behind us appeared endless. From the center, I couldn't see a single one of the white-robed priests we had walked past on our way in. Across the altar from us, the view was the same. To our right, the entire first row was comprised of malades on stretchers, attending

Mass in what might be the only basilica in the world designed to easily accommodate a hospital bed.

We were next to a middle-aged woman in a wheelchair, and behind another man in a wheelchair who had limited movement and speech. Our neighbors were all non-English-speaking and overjoyed to see a baby. Once again, it became evident to us that the primary purpose of Oscar's pilgrimage was to spread joy everywhere he went. They turned to crane their heads, cooing sweet baby nothings in their many languages.

The woman sitting next to me was attended by a Dame of Malta, who adjusted her blanket. Then she turned to Oscar, bent down, and gave him a long, divine smile—her gaze overflowing with peaceful love, a love in perfect contemplation of its desired object. It was the gaze of the lover upon his beloved.

All at once, I got it. I got why everyone was so drawn to Oscar, everywhere we went. Not just on this pilgrimage, but every day of his entire life. Oscar was Christ to others by offering himself as a receptacle to the spectacular, generous servant love on display here. The Knights and Dames, in turn, served as Christ to him with their hands and their feet, feeding, clothing, bathing, carrying him. But they also served as Christ to him with their eyes, just by the simple act of gazing at him—and at every malade here—with the same adoring love that we turn upon the Blessed Sacrament in adoration.

The lover and the beloved. The servant and the sick. The Christian and Christ. The exchange of love between God the Father and God the Son is the engine that creates God the Holy Spirit. Everywhere in the universe where that exchange of love is taking place, the Holy Spirit is brought forth anew. Anywhere that someone recognizes Christ within another and stops to look, love is reborn between them.

This foreign Dame, gazing upon her malade and then upon my son, was sitting in contemplation of the divine. In them, she approached and encountered her beloved, Jesus Christ. But the reverse was also true: Christ was present to her. By coming on the pilgrimage to receive the gift of service, the malades offered themselves as an icon of Christ—a tremendous and vulnerable gift of self to their attendants.

I now saw why Oscar and the other children were even more powerful than most malades: because they were innocent, without guile or baggage, Christ could shine through them more easily.

No wonder faces turned and lit every time Oscar passed. They were bathed with the light of Christ shining through the broken places in our little boy.

With a roar of organ thunder, Mass began. The pageantry was breathtaking. The processional hymn was a repetitive, hypnotic shout of praise: "All the earth, sing with joy to the Lord, alleluia!" The song began in French, and nearly every repetition of the chorus was in a new language, a dizzying array of sounds blending together, but always the meaning was the same. A tremendous line of flags, each representing a different Malta Association present at the pilgrimage, made its way up the center aisle.

After the flags, the deacons and priests began to process. And process. And process. When it seemed as if they had been at this for ten full minutes, I turned my head to look back down the aisle, and I still could not make out the end of the line. The sight of their flowing white robes, amid the riotous singing, made me picture an endless procession of angels and saints walking to the throne of God and casting their crowns at his feet. Finally, the last priests stepped up, and I turned again, thinking the procession was over. Instead, bringing up the rear were the bishops, archbishops, and cardinals. Even their line stretched for the entire length of the basilica, from the center altar to the outermost edge. I was suddenly certain that here was a depth of faith against which the gates of hell could never prevail.

If these are, in fact, the last remnants of Christianity in the world, I thought, *maybe we don't have much to fear after all.*

The cavernous room felt warm and alive, womb-like, as if we were cradled inside the very ribs of the Blessed Mother. What had looked and felt barren upon approach was no longer barren: it was filled with her children, gloriously fruitful. The evocation of ribs, of an upside-down ark, of being held inside Mary, were all fully intended, a nod to Mary's honorific title, the Ark of the New Covenant. The original Ark held the Ten Commandments, the tangible, physical sign of God's covenant with Israel. Mary held within her body the tangible, physical sign of God's New Covenant with the world: the person of Jesus Christ, God incarnate. The basilica's very design was yet another homage to Mary.

As the Mass continued, the sense of might, indestructibility, and universality increased. While this sense might be evoked at Mass in other holy places in Christendom—St. Peter's Basilica in Rome, for example—here it happened despite the bleak surroundings, without the benefit of eye-catching stained glass or marble floors. Flags, capes, incense, and pageantry notwithstanding, Mass was stripped down to its essence. No one was there to enjoy the utilitarian view of jumbotrons and pillars. Everyone was there because it is where Jesus was.

We had traveled across the world because we needed Jesus, and if he was going to show up at Mass in a hole, so were we.

The altar was in the very center of the room. Surrounding the altar on three sides were the sick, the lame, the blind, the cancerous, the downtrodden and dispossessed. They came in voitures, in wheelchairs, on stretchers. The places of highest honor were reserved for the least of the brethren. Anywhere else, such a sorry display of the frailty of human flesh might have seemed pitiful. Here, that frailty united to one another and to Christ had unfathomable power. Rather than marring the grand pageantry of the Mass, the presence of the broken, disabled, and despairing elevated the Mass to something even more sacred. Malades had walked, rolled, and crawled to get there. Some people, like the pilgrims from Syria and Lebanon, had clawed and fought their way there. From all corners of the world, the broken people came together as one body, to surround and lift up the Eucharist, the source and summit of our faith.

During the eucharistic prayer, the congregation responded in Latin. Among Catholics, there is a fairly strong and even bitter divide between those who pray in Latin and those who do not. Here in Lourdes, though, Latin was commingled comfortably with a dozen or more native languages. We prayed together in Latin not out of elitism but out of necessity: it was the shared mother tongue of our shared faith. While national identity was fully present and celebrated in the uniforms, flags, and multilingual hymns, Latin allowed every Catholic present to pray in unison. It was the language that set us apart as a people from the rest of the world.

We were jammed into this cold, damp cave, but my body felt suffused by warmth. At the sign of peace, every face beamed as people shook hands with each other and offered words of peace in native tongues. This happy cacophony provided a tiny glimpse of what a peaceful world might look like, so many cultures and languages and national hang-ups giving way to hands extended in open friendship. In the next moment, unity restored itself, as *Peace, Paz, Paix, Friede,* gave way again to one voice: *Agnus Dei, qui tollis peccata mundi . . .*

Every Sunday at Mass, I recite the words "one, holy, Catholic, and apostolic" in reference to the Church. Never before had I understood the unwavering, unassailable truth of those words. Here, truly, was one shepherd, one flock. Here, the last were first. Here was the Church as the Body of Christ made manifest. Here, the suffering were held closest to his Sacred Heart. Just as everyone had promised me, just as Scripture promises: Christ is close to those who suffer. I had never quite been able to fathom the meaning until I saw how the suffering were carried and cared for here, lowered through the roof onto Christ's very lap by their brothers and sisters in faith.

17.

CRÊPES AU CHOCOLAT

Our pod was crammed together at a too-small table in a cafe that was packed with Malta uniforms, inside and out. We had shoved Oscar's stroller in through the crowded maze of chairs to a corner where the only hope of getting him out again would be to lift him overhead. It felt cozy to be all together, our little surrogate family.

Our server came over and stared down at us imperiously, wordlessly, pencil in hand. An awkward silence stretched on. Oh, he wanted our order.

"Une crêpe au chocolat et un cappuccino, s'il vous plaît," I began, super proud of myself for ordering in French. He replied with a curt nod, unimpressed.

Amy ordered another crêpe, and then Kim. The server looked up from his notepad, visibly annoyed. He said something in rapid French, but all I could make out was something along the lines of "I thought you were here to eat." I did my best to reassure him, totally confused about why crêpes on plates eaten with knife and fork didn't count. Todd ordered a salad to placate him (and possibly keep us from getting summarily ejected). When he left, we snickered about what had been the week's only example of stereotypically haughty French customer service. *Très* un-Lourdes-like.

I turned to Kim, ready with the question that was the reason we were all gathered here, apart from the hotel and our four-hundred-person entourage. "Okay, please tell me what you saw during my bath with Oscar. I hardly remember anything, almost like my mind is blocking out trauma." I had been waiting anxiously for this conversation for two days.

Most of the distinct steps Kim described were in line with the broken images in my mind. As she talked, my own memories came into sharper focus, as if I were rewatching a movie that I had seen while half-asleep. I nodded along, sometimes closing my eyes; it was hard to know whether I was remembering or constructing new memories as she spoke.

She described lowering Oscar into the water, she and I together, his cry and his forceful, spasm-like movement. The agony of that moment stabbed my chest again like a hot knife; I was still inwardly berating myself for subjecting him to that. She told how she lifted him higher, pulling him close to her chest, and instructed me to take some water out of the bath with my hand and put it on his head.

"Oh, I remember that!" I exclaimed. "I remember thinking, 'I don't want any more of this damn water to touch him, ever again.' I almost couldn't bring myself to do it."

Kim's eyes glittered at me, and she nodded. "But you did. And it was like he . . . ," she paused, looking for the right expression, "absolutely melted. The minute that water touched his head, he relaxed and put his head down on my shoulder, and he was calm. Then he started looking around, and his eyes were bright and curious. It was instantaneous. It was amazing."

I looked at her, overcome, unable to speak for a long beat. "But I don't remember that. He was crying."

She shook her head vehemently. "No. He didn't cry at all from that moment forward, the rest of the time he was in the baths. The hospitallers came to get him dressed while I helped you, and he was perfectly calm the whole time. I will never forget that moment as long as I live. He melted."

I had missed the transformation she witnessed. My heart had been so aching with worry that I had missed our first miracle. I looked around the table, and Carole's eyes were wet. Todd reached across and squeezed my hand.

"I don't remember that. I didn't see it," I murmured, with no small regret. "It was like an out-of-body experience. I just wanted to get out of there. When I came out, I could barely form sentences."

Carole nodded. "Yes, you were very quiet. We were a little worried about you."

"I just felt tired," I told her. "I didn't want to think, or talk, or really be around anyone. I was just done."

"What about you, Todd?" Amy asked. "What was your bath like?"

"They split us up right at the beginning, so Christy and Oscar went to the women's and children's side and I went to the men's." His words came out almost before Amy had finished asking the question. Todd processes the world by explaining it out loud. He had been waiting eagerly for this moment; I read that much on his face. I felt a pang of guilt that it hadn't even occurred to me to ask him this question anytime in the last two days.

"When I went in, I was put in a line about fifteen or twenty people away from the door," he continued. "At the very front there were a lot of men on stretchers. I just sat where they told me and started following the Rosary. I started thinking about what I was bringing to the baths, what I was bringing to Lourdes.

He paused and looked at me, as if deciding whether to say the next thing on his lips. "I didn't have all these expectations like Christy did." I looked down at my crêpe and began to cut another bite, pointedly, then glanced over to check on Oscar, who was napping peacefully, to avoid meeting my husband's gaze.

"So, I just sat there and prayed and stopped listening to what was going on. For some period of time, I just prayed, 'God, heal my son if it's your will. Help my wife, if it's your will,' in a rote kind of way. But all of a sudden I heard a question. I heard God ask me, *Tell me what you really, really, really want. What is that thing deep in your heart? What do you need and want?*"

He swallowed, hard. "I burst out crying like a baby, and I said, 'Lord, I want you to heal my family.' I didn't even know what that meant. The kids? Our issues? All the fighting? You and I and our stuff?" He flicked his eyes in my direction again. "I just totally broke down. I mean, I was ugly crying. I probably repeated myself a hundred times, 'Lord, I want you to heal my family.' Then they called me inside the door."

The table was dead quiet. Everyone had stopped eating, put down their forks, just listening intently. Todd is a gifted, natural storyteller, and this was one of those pivotal stories you know helps to define the shape of a life.

"When I got inside, I was overwhelmed. I didn't know what to do. Most of the hospitallers were gruff and busy, but one had an incredibly kind face, just total gentleness. He looked over at me, and I swear he looked into my soul. Then he said, 'Hold on,' to a bunch of people in front of me and took me first.

"I started changing, and for whatever reason, this guy had taken some interest in me, taken me under his wing. I sat there, alone in my underwear. But I felt like that man was my guide, that I wasn't by myself. I told him my wife and son were in the other bath, and he told me, 'Now is the time for you to just be. You're not in a hurry. Take a minute to pray. We'll pray with you.'"

Not a single person interrupted Todd's story to ask questions. I was remembering the scene inside the baths, the concrete, the plastic chairs, the striped curtains, all the confusion and trauma that had been coursing through my body. It seemed a bluntly clinical setting for such profound encounters with the divine and with the self. A lot of Lourdes was like that, now that I came to think of it—the underground basilica, the brutally modernist chapel.

I grieved to think of Todd, completely broken down, sitting alone on a plastic lawn chair among strangers. I grieved more to think of him sitting alone in our living room while I purposely sat somewhere—anywhere—else, as I'd done all year. If he'd felt alone in the baths, he'd not lacked for practice at aloneness. I marveled, ruefully, that Todd had had yet another life-altering spiritual experience that I had not been part of, known about, or talked about. In my husband's own Gethsemane, God had sent an angel to minister to him, as Kim had intervened in mine. But we had not been each other's angels, not for a while.

"I prayed again, 'God, please heal my family,'" Todd went on. "I looked at the men, nodded, and we said an Our Father and a Hail

Mary together. We walked down in there, and Our Lady was right in front of me, the statue. I think I said, 'Thank you.' They dunked me down in, splashed my face, and I took a drink. Then we turned around and started coming out.

"I don't know that I felt a lot different immediately. I felt like I had done the right thing. It was right that I had gone through that. This wasn't a wasted thing for me to have done. All I remember is breaking down, being in a place where I had no idea what was going on, and that angel of a hospitaller. There wasn't a tissue box anywhere. This is not the way that men handle that experience, I'm sure," he laughed. "And then I came out and found Christy sitting in the voiture with Oscar and Ryan and everyone else. I didn't feel like I could talk, then."

Kim reassured him, "Lots of men cry. It's not just you."

"No one was crying like I was," Todd responded with his trademark wry grin. I had always loved his ability to poke fun of himself.

Amy chimed in, "I'm going tomorrow morning. After these stories, I can't wait to see what happens."

"Something always does," Kim answered. "Everyone gets what they need." Carole nodded, decisively, as if that settled the question.

18.

IN THE FOOTSTEPS OF BERNADETTE

A short while later we stood with a crowd in front of the Boly Mill in the heart of the village. This was the first stop on a walking tour to visit several landmarks in Bernadette's everyday life before the apparitions. Walking across the bridge to the other side of town, away from the Domain and all its churches and chanting, felt like an escape. The streets on the other side of town were lined not just with Catholic religious memorabilia shops, but with beautiful antiques and handicrafts, small supermarkets, and open-front restaurants hawking sandwiches and kebabs. Suddenly we were on vacation, not on pilgrimage.

The Boly Mill was the home of the Soubirous family when Bernadette was born. Her father was then a miller in town, fully employed and well able to provide for his family's needs. The plastered rooms of the museum were neat, trim, and comfortable. Inside, pictures showed what it would have been like in the 1840s: crumpled and careworn, but serviceable. A handout explained that the family had to leave the mill because M. Soubirous gradually fell into debt. But all historical accounts agree that the Boly Mill was a happy home for Bernadette and that her family was loving and devout.

After being evicted from the mill, the family was offered a basement room in a building owned by a relative. This room, known as the *cachot*, is where Bernadette lived at the time of the apparition. "Room" is a generous descriptor; previously, it had been used as a prison, until it was condemned as unhealthy and unfit for prisoners and given to pigs instead. The Soubirous family was in such desperate straits that they reclaimed it as a living space from the pigs. The family of six squeezed themselves into the 170 square feet of the *cachot*, which literally means "dungeon." Bernadette's asthma was greatly exacerbated by the fetid, dank air.

We stepped down a dark anteroom displaying some of Bernadette's belongings into the cachot itself. The room was bright and simple, with clean yellow plaster, a slate floor, and gorgeous wood beams in the ceiling, the total effect conveying the kind of rustic farmhouse chic that people in America pay a lot of money to imitate. While the space was spotless now, it was not hard to imagine what it would have been like with moldy floors and stale air. And it was tiny. We crammed in about twenty people at a time, with hardly room enough to stand and turn around. Our own house is small by American standards, and I sometimes despaired at the awkwardness of our den—which is to say our second, *extra* living room—but that den was easily twice as large as this, the entire living space for Bernadette's family of six.

As we exited the cachot (easily accomplished by taking four or five steps to the right), we were met with a display of photographs and quotes from Bernadette's official testimony about the apparitions, translated into various languages. One jumped out at me:

Ce que j'ai vu et entendu . . . je suis chargée de vous le dire,
je ne suis pas chargée de vous le faire croire.

I am entrusted with telling you what I have seen and heard.
I am not entrusted with making you believe it.

The guide in the *cachot* mentioned that Bernadette had never been healed of her asthma or tuberculosis, both of which eventually contributed to her death. Even embarking on the path to sainthood, even having been graced with the gift of a vision of the Mother of God, even partaking of the water of Lourdes, which her own hands dug out of the earth—Bernadette was never cured. She lived a hard, short life. In fact, during one of the apparitions, the "beautiful lady" spelled it out for Bernadette with unmistakable clarity: "I do not promise to make you happy in this world, but in the other." I was moved by Bernadette's quiet defiance and steadfastness in the face of her hardships, so different from my crumpling, tissue-paper heart. She did not complain, nor did she back down from the enormity of the task before her. She stood before the town magistrate and the clergy and testified. She held her ground, even under harsh questioning. Then she retired into a life of seclusion, suffered, and died.

That quote burrowed itself instantly into my heart, a seed so deeply planted that I couldn't root it out if I tried. God was entrusting me with the task of telling what I had seen and heard on this pilgrimage. I had started writing a blog before we left, attempting to untangle my labyrinthine thoughts in public words; it now seemed this was no accident. The pilgrimage would not be the epilogue to those anguished musings, but the next beginning. And I knew that God would not remove this cross. The mission was clear to me now. Raise this kid, as he is created, and tell people about what you have seen and heard.

The only thing left to me to decide was this: How would I respond?

Before returning to our hotel, we made one last stop at the local parish church, which contained the font where Bernadette had been baptized. There, as a group, we renewed our own baptismal vows. God was putting a seal on the things he had just revealed, to secure my promise of trust to this new deal he was offering me.

"Do you reject Satan?"

I do. I reject Satan. Get thee behind me. You have no power over me anymore.

"And all his works?"

I do. I reject the temptations and lies he has planted in my mind and my heart. I reject his falsehood that to be worthy you must be perfect.

"And all his empty promises?"

I do. I reject his promise that despair is a viable way out.

"Do you believe in God, the Father Almighty, creator of heaven and earth?"

I do. I believe that he is there, that he is listening, and that he loves me as he loved Bernadette, as he loves Oscar.

"Do you believe in Jesus Christ, his only Son, our Lord, who was born of the Virgin Mary, was crucified, died, and was buried, rose from the dead, and is now seated at the right hand of the Father?"

I do. I believe that there is value in our suffering, as there was value in his. I believe that pouring out your life in service is never wasted.

"Do you believe in the Holy Spirit, the holy Catholic Church, the communion of saints, the forgiveness of sins, the resurrection of the body, and life everlasting?"

I do. Oh, I do. I believe in the simple strength of Bernadette. I believe that the Blessed Mother is praying for my son right now, and for Todd, and for me. I believe that the Holy Spirit can console any sorrow of any size, and that the Church is a living collection of people who can offer the care and healing of Christ through their very own hands.

I believe that God forgives me my despair.

B ack at the hotel, we encountered our next little miraculous gift. During each of my pregnancies, some family or another had stepped forward to support our family in important, critically necessary, and usually surprising ways. In each case, it seemed as if God was hand-selecting our children's godparents. Kim and Peter Barger lived near us, and our daughters were in school together—the more logistical help Kim and Peter gave us, the more spiritual encouragement they provided too.

For several years, Peter had been in formation to become a permanent deacon for the Diocese of Austin. Deacons can do many of the pastoral things a priest can do: witness a marriage, baptize, preside at funerals, preach, and teach. They can't forgive sins or consecrate the host, but they are ordained clergy and spiritual coleaders in most other meaningful ways. For her part, Kim was incredibly active in women's ministry in our parish and diocese.

After Oscar got sick, we discovered another of the Bargers' gifts: the gift of intercessory prayer for the healing of others. This child, who so desperately needed prayers, was awash in them. The Bargers' powerful, prayerful presence in Oscar's stormy life, from before he was even born, was entirely providential.

So was the fact that the Bargers were waiting for us in our hotel lobby when we returned from the Footsteps of Bernadette tour.

Peter and Kim were in the middle of another pilgrimage with deacon candidates and clergy from Austin, visiting religious sites in Italy, France, and Portugal. The Lourdes portion of their pilgrimage overlapped directly with ours. They had had their tickets long before we had even thought about, let alone applied for, let alone been accepted to, the Order of Malta pilgrimage. Before our own travel plans materialized, the Bargers had already promised to pray for Oscar's healing at every stop along their trip. Now, here in Lourdes, we would pray for it together.

I barely managed to keep from jumping up and down as I ran to hug Peter and Kim. (Okay, no, I didn't manage. I also admit that I squealed.) It felt absolutely, phenomenally impossible that they were here, providing credible evidence that this spiritual fantasyland was an actual place in the real world. It now contained people we knew. Grounded in the physical, tangible presence of our real-life friends, gears in my brain clicked forward. As I hugged Peter and Kim, trusting their bodies, I trusted even more that what was happening to us was really happening, that this pilgrimage experience was not all just some fanciful, curious dream.

We sat down in the lobby for coffee and cocktails, and I was about to get my first practice at telling, following Bernadette's example, what we had seen and heard.

Peter and Kim leaned over Oscar's stroller and cooed at him. "Hi, Oscar! How is your trip?" Most of the time, trying to have a conversation with Oscar was a futile, even boring, experience. Obviously, he couldn't talk, but quite often he would give you exactly zero social response: no eye contact, no smile, no cute baby gurgles or babbles. Today, though, as his godparents reached down to kiss his fat cheeks and rub his wispy hair, he smiled brightly and followed them with his eyes. When they stopped talking, he kicked his legs and slapped his hands up and down on the bar in front of him, with an "Ooo-ooo-ooo!" To look at him, you'd have thought he was trying to elicit another round of kisses, but that couldn't be.

Peter looked up at me with his eyes full of wonder. "He looks amazing."

"He does, doesn't he? Everyone has been saying how different he is, but I didn't really see it until now, seeing him with you." I spoke carefully, looking at Oscar, not at Peter.

Phone in hand, Peter snapped a couple of photos, then turned the screen to show me. Oscar smiled with his whole body, arm mid-swing, eyes sharp with intent, mouth curved upward slightly more on one side than the other—Todd's smile. His gorgeous, doughy-round cheek sported a heavy dimple, just like his father's. I could probably count on one hand the number of photos we had of Oscar smiling like this—they were few and far between, and he was always smiling at something or someone else in the frame, never just hamming it up for the camera lens.

"Look at him! This is amazing. He's like a different kid," Peter said beaming.

In the dining room, we settled down to enjoy the standard daily four-course dinner. *Vive la France!* What a relief it was to have a tiny bit of distance from "pilgrimage brain." We talked about our respective trips, of course, but with our dear friends, I didn't have to expend the mental energy to grope for small talk, in addition to processing the spiritual growth of the last five days. In *Bread and Wine*, her love letter to food, community, and hospitality, Shauna Niequist reminds us that "food matters because it's one of the things that forces us to live in this world—this tactile, physical, messy, and beautiful world—no matter how hard we try to escape into our minds and our ideals."[1] The breaking of bread with old friends around the table that day grounded my soul in a way that had been slowly taking hold all week. I felt solid again, instead of the wraithlike self I had brought to Lourdes, that wounded ghost walking through the unreal landscape of my deformed life.

Catholicism is a religion of the tangible. Bread. Wine. Oil. Water. These physical gifts are the instruments through which God pours his grace into the world, especially through the hands of other people. Everything about this day seemed specially designed to highlight the universality of that experience, even the purely metaphysical truths behind them. The sustenance I received in the Eucharist, or shared with a team I had just met, or passed from hand to hand with my son's godparents five thousand miles away from our home—the source of all these gifts was the same divine love. They were the physical proof of that love, in the same way that my son's very existence was. God was whispering to my heart, "I am here. You can trust me. This is real."

I thought back to Oscar, the child who was born on the Sabbath day, and his *bonny and blithe, good and gay*, very real smile for Peter's camera. Maybe I could trust that, too, I realized. Maybe that was not a fluke.

19.

SEALED WITH THE GIFTS

The next morning we returned to the Rosary Basilica, the site of Thursday's opening Tri-Association Mass, this time for Monday's closing Mass. As the charioteers lined up the voitures along the front, I listened to the idle chitchat around me and overheard that Billy and Thomas were going to be confirmed that day. Billy was Joyce's son, and Thomas was Steve's son—the two parents from our caregiver reflection group!

Confirmation seals us with the gift of the Holy Spirit, the culmination and fulfillment of our baptismal promises. In a Catholic infant baptism, those promises are made by parents and godparents, as we had done for Oscar. As children grow, and learn to think and speak for themselves, they renew those promises periodically, as we had done the day before in the Lourdes parish church. But at Confirmation, the baptized renew these promises publicly, sealed by grace through the hands of the bishop, who anoints the newly confirmed with sacred oil. Like all sacraments, it is both visible and invisible, an outward sign of inward grace.

I loved the sacrament of Confirmation. My favorite Mass of every year is the Easter Vigil, a three-hour, full-choir, trumpets-and-incense affair after sundown, in the soul-stifling darkness just before Easter morning when the whole world holds its breath, culminating in a riotous cacophony of Baptisms, Confirmations, and First Communions by the dozen in the middle of the service. Because Todd and I had both been confirmed together in our twenties through the Rite of

Christian Initiation of Adults (RCIA) at an Easter Vigil, I remembered
our Confirmation vividly.

At the time, I had been noticeably pregnant with our first child,
the daughter who would seal us with the gift of parenthood forever.
We stood on the steps before the handmade wooden altar of our
tiny church, the Catholic Student Center at the university where we
attended graduate school. We were surrounded by many of those
faithful, honest people who had wrestled graciously with our theological questions and intellectual arguments, and whose patient forth-
rightness had eventually helped to win our conversion. That beautiful
Easter Vigil Mass was the first I had ever attended, though I had been
Catholic since birth. Through hours of readings and the chanting
of Psalms, we sat in hot, heavy darkness, and when the lights were
thrown on, the doors of my heart flew open. The anointing of my
head with balsam-scented chrism oil was a powerful, tender, and
holy experience, even more so because I had the honor of standing
alongside my husband as he received his own anointing seconds later.
I remember the smiles we gave each other, how the scent lingered
for days, how we glowed with candlelight and sacredness, our hearts
joined in a new way forever.

Before me, in this holy place of Lourdes, these two boys, Billy
and Thomas, would receive this grace standing under the dome of
the basilica of Our Lady of the Rosary. All the while, that bejeweled,
teenaged Mother of God on the ceiling would shine down upon them,
glittering gold and glory. Like all churches, this was God's house, but
it was wrapped in Mary's mantle, built on her hallowed ground.

The voitures were packed in so tightly in the front of the church
that there was no room to walk between. Oscar and I were sand-
wiched between faces that were, by this point in the week, familiar and
beloved. Contentment settled like a blanket over us, while a pleasant
hum of conversation thrummed along underneath. This group of
suffering individuals had arrived defensive and careworn, but our
tightly clutched fingers-in-fists had been pried apart, knotted knuckles
cracked open, woven inextricably back together through the days of
pilgrimage, long but few. We were woven with prayer and tears and

hope. We were woven with hands anointed and bread broken and lives poured out for each other.

We would never again be alone in our suffering.

I smiled over my shoulder at Todd and the Bargers. We all have moments when our worlds collide, when a coworker dates your cousin or your college roommate moves in next door to your daughter's best friend. Seeing the friends of our hometown seated among the Order of Malta pilgrims, street clothes bounded by the ocean of black-and-red uniforms, there was no awkwardness. It felt as if they had been here with us all along. They had supported us so closely with their prayers all year that, in a way, they *had* been here with us all along. Into my mind sprang St. Peter's words to Jesus on the mountaintop, when Moses and Elijah appeared before them: "Lord, it is good that we are here." We were here, on our own mountaintop, and it was so, so good.

As the strains of the opening hymn began to thunder through the soaring vault of the dome, I turned to watch the procession. At its head, Elizabeth's son Matthias, her anxious little malade who had begun the week looking haunted and wan, calmly led the phalanx of priests. He was garbed in the black cassock and intricate white surplice of an altar server. His hands were neatly folded, his eyes clear and placid.

And that was it. That was God's last nudge, the last thing it took. At the sight of Matthias, restored by active, unconditional love and shrouded in community, the dam burst. I began to cry, laying down my stubborn prickliness and distrust in total and final surrender. Love always wins, always. Always and always, I understood now, in *kairos* and *chronos—nunc, et semper, et in saecula saeculorum,* now, and always, and forever and ever. *Amen.* So be it.

You cannot fight love. And why, in the name of all things holy and right and good, had I ever, ever wanted to?

Oscar had been especially lively that morning, increasingly impatient with the voiture. He squirmed as I cried, oblivious to my emotional breakthrough, disgruntled and downright feisty about being confined to my lap. I handed him one toy after another, but he threw down every last one with an indignant squawk, each louder than the one before. It appeared that, at long last, the worst-case scenario of

Kim Gillespie—Dame of Malta, pod host, and preplanner extraordi-
naire—was finally coming true: Oscar was losing his marbles during
Mass, and I was completely trapped in the middle of an immovable
pack of voitures with him shouting at the top of his lungs.

This had actually never happened during a Mass with him before.
Ever. We had a perfectly compliant one-and-a-half-year-old boy.
"You're so lucky that he's so good during Mass!" people would praise
him. "Thanks!" I would answer cheerfully, while glowering inwardly,
"That's because that's all he can do." I was eating my words today. This
kid was raising hell.

A pair of open hands extended over my shoulder. As I turned, I
saw the malade behind me was waiting to hand Oscar to Todd and the
Bargers in the row behind him. We passed Oscar back like a full (and
very wiggly) bucket in a fire brigade, and he moved back and forth
among their laps, fussy then soothed, active then still. They took turns
enfolding him in their arms, a tiny community easing his tiny, ordinary toddler sufferings. No suffering in Lourdes is ever borne alone.

For this Mass, I was the malade, sitting alone in our voiture,
wounded, bearing permanent scars, but already healing.

When the time came for the Rite of Confirmation, Steve stood
behind Thomas's wheelchair, hand resting on his son's shoulder, the
man who felt so abandoned and betrayed by his community now lifted
up by his new one. Joyce stepped forward, nudging Billy gently into
place; he was about to be sealed as a full adult in the faith. In one fell
swoop, I realized how fearful I had been about Oscar's future path, not
just in ordinary life but also in the Church; in the exact same moment,
I realized those fears had been answered before I had even given them
a name. He could do it. He could receive all these sacraments. If Billy
could, Oscar could. Even if the wider world defined him by his brokenness—even if I myself had long defined him that way—Oscar was
a whole, worthy person in the eyes of God and the Church.

At Communion, my own wide-open, wide-awake heart received
Jesus, as my mouth received the tiny, unremarkable host. I was so in
love with Jesus, all over again, marveling at what he had done: that
his mother and this place and these people had somehow brought
me back to him.

20.

LIFE WINS

After Mass, we transferred Oscar to his stroller so he could go home for a nap with Malta-Kim (not to be confused with god-mother-Kim). I had joked to Todd earlier in the week about the coincidence (providence!) that most of our pod members had names that already had great significance in Oscar's life. His two Kims, both wry and prayerful and mysteriously present exactly where and when we needed them. Carole, the friendly Malta grandmother, and Carole, the friendly physical therapist grandmother, each supportive and encouraging but shot through with practical strength. Amy Cattapan, kindred spirit of the week, and my own Amy, best friend and soul sister of my life, who had vicariously shouldered so much of my grief this year.

The Bargers, Todd, and I trudged up the stairs on one side of the Rosary Basilica. On a hill high above the Domain, our group would pray the Stations of the Cross together, a spiritual walk through the crucifixion of Jesus, from his humiliating public sentencing to his brutal, agonizing walk to his death, and to the stone enclosing his body in the tomb. At each station, a meditation is offered that helps us enter more deeply into the mystery of suffering and the even bigger mystery of redemption. There are many kinds of narrative prayers like this in the Catholic Church—the other most notable one being the Rosary itself, which walks twenty episodes of Jesus' life seen through the eyes of Mary. I love the way these narratives connect to epic, primal human experience. Even if you don't believe in Christ, everyone has been wrongly accused and knows what that feels like. Everyone has felt crushed by the weight of a burden. Everyone has failed at something so that it seemed as if there was no way forward.

We climbed further, up a green hill shrouded in trees and paved in gravel. Before we had even reached the first station, I was winded. The experienced Knights and Dames had warned us that this would be an arduous climb, and I was beginning to wonder if my long days as a stay-at-home mother, my sole exercise chasing kids from room to room and squatting to change diapers, had been an adequate training regimen for this excursion. I glanced around and noticed several senior citizens and several malades who appeared to be having no trouble whatsoever with this level of activity. I refused to be bested in a show of athleticism by the sick and the elderly, but I did also glance around to see if there was a picturesque stone wall somewhere against which I could casually lean to catch my breath. (There was.)

Once the Stations began, though, my feebleness left my thoughts, replaced by the story unfolding before my eyes as we wound uphill, deeper into the Pyrenean forest. These "Upper Stations" (a shorthand moniker to distinguish them from the "Lower Stations" on a grassy plain near the grotto) are composed of dazzling bronze statues, standing larger than life, cast with lyrical expressiveness and movement in their bodies but with empty eyes, lacking irises or pupils. They were both human and not human, relatable and alien, in the same way that the story itself is both us and not-us, man and God.

Our pilgrim group was solemn, a weird gladness in the solemnity. The mysteries we were pondering together were the weightiest matters faced by any human who ever lived: condemnation, torture, execution. Simultaneously, our hearts were alive with love. The wild resplendence of the day was hard to ignore. Above us, the sky soared deep into an otherworldly blue; the leaves around us rustled with life and song, while before us, Christ was being stripped and beaten into submission.

Every day, people suffered, and the sun shone anyway. People died, and the birds still sang.

One, two, three: Jesus was condemned, accepted his cross, and fell to his knees under its unyielding weight. At the fourth station, the priest leading the meditations (the same one I had accosted just two days ago) announced, "Jesus meets his sorrowful mother," and my ears pricked up. In all this year of asking and begging and praying, it had never really sunk in with me that Mary had not only watched her son die but had watched him *suffer* first. She, too, had watched something happen to her precious child that she was powerless to stop. I had held my son through his traumatic, awful seizures, held him as he wailed in pain he couldn't understand or explain to us. In those terrible moments, I felt alone and abandoned, even unnatural. How could anyone bear to watch a child suffer like this? Such pain seemed a violation of the deepest structures of nature itself.

Mary had endured watching her son suffer before I ever had.

Father read, "As Mary greets her son, her grace-filled face blesses his mission."

I have been saying all week that Oscar's mission on this pilgrimage is to bring joy to people, I mused. *But what is his mission in life? What has been written on my face this year?* Without needing to admit it, I knew that his mission in life was the same. This child was born to be a beacon of joy. Everyone he met wanted to touch him, to say hello and just be close to him. So many malades had begged to just have him on their laps for a moment in their voitures.

I knew, also, that my face had been full of neither grace nor blessing. Mary had stood before her son in the final moments of his life, knowing that he was about to be murdered in cold blood before an angry mob, and her grace-filled face blessed his final mission. Perhaps I could manage to muster a smile in the face of our troubles from time to time.

Four, five, six. We pilgrims grew steadily calmer, quieter, as our feet crunched along the choppy stone path: fewer side conversations, less murmuring. The everyday world seemed to be falling away behind us, the rhythm of our steps elevating us further into the cloud of unknowing, into contemplation.

At the seventh station, Jesus falls a second time, utterly unable to cope with the weight that has been handed to him. Our chaplain spoke of the "poverty of not being able to be self-reliant. Jesus was deprived of the satisfaction of carrying this cross on his own." I thought about

how much I had tried to do on my own this year, and how satisfying—how bitterly, spitefully satisfying!—it was to be self-reliant in
managing Oscar's care and our chaotic family life. From the moment
of his first seizure, I had wanted to do it alone, almost refusing a nun
who asked to hold and comfort him.

How initially painful, and how eventually sweet, it was to allow
our family to just be helped during our time in Lourdes. People asked
and asked and asked to help us here, and I said no, until I couldn't
say no anymore; if my pride had not caused me to say yes to help,
just to avoid ruining someone else's vacation, I would have said no
until I collapsed, too spent to go on. I understood how much Jesus
would have wanted to carry the cross up that hill by himself. He truly
could not, and so he had to bear the suffering of both the cross and
his irrefutable powerlessness to carry it alone. The cross was never
meant to be borne alone.

By the time we reached the crucifixion station, with the bronze
corpus of Jesus soaring high above us among the treetops, the strug-
gle of the climb had integrated itself into the whole experience of the
stations. We had not just prayed them; we had walked them, lived
them. So much else in Lourdes had been about sitting and listening,
or sitting and talking, or sitting and praying, but now we were praying
with the struggling breath of our bodies and the aching soles of our
feet. With the aid of the priest's meditations, it felt as if we had accompanied Christ on his walk and were now staring at his bloodied self,
hanging and dying in agony over our heads. No one spoke. Moving
downhill now, we stepped to the next station, where Mary received
the broken body of her only son.

The walk after that was a longer one, and pensive. The silence
was broken by our priest announcing the final station, the fourteenth:
"Jesus is placed in the tomb." He described how friends and disciples
had run away and how Jesus was buried only by his mother and Joseph
of Arimathea, a secret disciple who donated his own new tomb to
the cause. There was no undoing what had been done. (There was no
undoing what had been done to all of us, either. It just was. The fact
of it existed.)

After a short pause, Father asked us to turn away from the statues in the tomb, to turn around and gaze out across the majestic landscape unrolling itself to the invisible horizon beyond the mountains. We turned together, Todd and I, his arm wrapped around my shoulder and my head resting on his chest.

"Death does not win. Life wins," Father said simply.

As we continued down the hill after praying the Stations, and I regained my equilibrium, we came upon a side path, labeled *Chemin de Consolation* (Path of Consolation), which led into a shrine inside a small cave. In the deepest recess, there she was.

The Pietà. My Pietà. Mary, the Blessed Mother, cradling the body of her dead son. This image of Mary's sorrow was one I had not dared to contemplate too closely for many months, not since the day in the adoration chapel when Jesus had spelled out with unmistakable clarity that the cross of Oscar's illness would not—would *never*—be taken away. That day, images of the Pietà had raged uncontrollably through my mind. I had seen the dirt on Jesus' skin, the blood pooling in the creases of his elbow. I had seen the tears and sweat streaked on Mary's face, their hair matted together as she leaned over him. And I had shut it out as firmly as I could in the interim, unable to bear even my own suffering, let alone the internal meditative experience of anyone else's.

The pilgrimage, though, had gradually brought me back to life. I had survived the year of trials with a heart of stone. God had been at his delicate work here, rebuilding a heart of flesh, cell by cell, muscle fiber by beating fiber. And today, at Mass, at Stations of the Cross, the tender new veins and arteries had been reconnected to the lifeblood of the Church: the suffering, triumphant Body of Christ. There was no shutting out suffering, or ignoring it, or working around it. The way out was straight through and into the very heart of it, but now I was ready, in a way I had not been ready before. This new heart, this heart of flesh—it was Mary's heart. She had given hers to me and hidden me inside hers. In that moment, the prayer of St. Teresa of Calcutta (Mother Teresa) became my own: "Mary, lend me your heart, and keep me in your most pure heart."[1]

Every year for the last six or seven years—well, except for the year of horrors just past—I had renewed a personal consecration to Mary using some variation of those words of Mother Teresa's. Consecration is a special devotion where you ask Mary to use you as God's instrument and help form you into a saint. Because she was conceived without sin (the Immaculate Conception), Mary is perfectly aligned with the will of God. Entrusting our lives to her means that we can be perfectly secure in the knowledge that she will help us align ourselves with God's will, too, nudging us along the straight and narrow path as mothers do.

Fr. Michael Gaitley, a priest with a great and holy devotion to Mary and a mission to spread that devotion, explained St. Teresa's quote even further. The prayer asks Mary to help us love everyone, most especially Jesus, in the perfect way that she loves; however, "to understand and live it," Fr. Gaitley continues, "requires a loving dependence and profound union with Mary."[2]

I felt both now, dependence and union, while kneeling before Mary, who carried her suffering in her arms, openly and without shame—a masterclass for the world on how to love, how to suffer because of that love, and how to let your heart still go on beating.

My consecration was complete.

Todd and I knelt to light a candle, clinging to each other, in tearful gratitude for the privilege of suffering with Mary. Chase and Megan, the young couple who had battled Megan's cancer with their infant in tow, stepped out of the shadows and stood beside us.

"Can we pray over you?" Megan asked. We managed to nod through our tears, and they each put a hand on our shoulders, supplication wrapping the four of us together.

"Father, we ask you to bless this family," Megan began. "You have given them a beautiful son, and they are such loving, good parents to him. Please bring healing to Oscar and to Todd and Christy, who are trying to live out your will with faith and trust."

This couple, who had lived through literal hell together, were here to minister to us. All of us pilgrims felt stronger, walked taller, than we had five days ago. No one who wasn't a true believer was likely to come to a major Catholic pilgrimage site on a journey seeking healing, but there had been a divide in my mind: the people who came to serve, and the people who came to be served. But here, now, were two people who had come to *be* served suddenly stepping over the line to join the other team.

Megan and Chase were stepping forward to meet us in the place of suffering. They knew the way to get down there, and we had all, together, begun to find our way out again, simply by taking each other's hands and not letting go.

We walked back toward town, pensive.

"I want to buy a Mary medal while we're here," said Todd.

"Let's check out that Bethlehem shop everyone keeps talking about."

Unlike many other shops in Lourdes that featured linoleum floors and tacky neon, the Bethlehem shop felt like a chapel unto itself. Dark and woody, the shop smelled of the shavings used to package and display the sculpted figurines and lovingly painted statues that were handcrafted by monasteries throughout the world.

I had never really known Todd to be a "Mary" guy. Mary can be a divisive figure for Christians, and even for Catholics. People either don't get what the big deal is, uncomfortable with the fact that she seems to be stealing some of Jesus' thunder ("Catholics worship Mary!"); or, on the flip side, they are totally on fire with devotion to her (lending credence to the cry "Catholics worship Mary!"). I was firmly "on fire," and had been almost since the instant I became a mother myself, because the mother-son relationship made intuitive sense to me. I knew it in my flesh and bones. As St. Maximilian Kolbe put it, "Never be afraid of loving the Blessed Virgin too much. You can never love her more than Jesus did." Whatever my issues with God and Jesus had been, I had never stopped loving Mary.

For his part, Todd didn't object to Mary; he just didn't see the need for her. Preferring to mediate his faith directly with God, Todd left Mary to the crazy veil-wearing housewives (like his own). That day, though, he spent over thirty minutes selecting just the right medal, a diminutive Mary surrounded by glowing stars and a deep field of hand-enameled blue. I had never seen anything like it before. As soon as he had paid, he tore off the tiny price tag, attached it to his chain, and put it on while we hurried to our parent reflection group.

The atmosphere in the room was markedly different this time. Whatever crazy love had knit the pilgrims together on the macro scale had worked in this little microcosm, too, not least of all because Joyce and Steve were still smiling from their sons' morning Confirmations.

Elizabeth set the tone this time, giving words to the feelings we all shared. "My children lived in perfect love this week, and they just blossomed." She explained in more detail about Matthias in particular, the little altar server—how at home he is normally withdrawn, temperamental, and extremely sensitive to changes in routine. She had been bracing for a hard week of managing his anxieties and physical challenges, but it hadn't materialized.

"The kids weren't seen here as their labels or problems but as who they truly are," she explained. "They were just children for a week." Instead of being seen as the sum of his diagnoses, Matthias was seen as a child of God, seen with the eyes of Christ. By the end of the week, being seen had healed his heart.

"They were just treated like kids here, not *special-needs* kids," Elizabeth went on. "That acceptance has made me see my kids in that way, too, instead of always thinking about them in terms of managing their medical needs."

Todd broke in, "For me, it's actually been about Mary. I never really understood her before. I didn't have a problem with her; I just didn't bother with her at all. But I get now what people mean when they say she is our mother—I mean, she is *literally* our mother. This week I feel like I was able to admit that what I need right now is a mother. Like, in the most basic, juvenile way—I skinned my knee and I want my mom!"

Everyone chuckled, but Todd was completely earnest. "No, I'm serious! I'm hurting, and I'm going through something hard, and what I really need is a mom. She's been here all along, but I just didn't know it. I know now how much Mama Mary loves me. And I really needed to be loved like that."

21.

OUR LADY OF LOURDES

Our pod host Kim volunteered to walk us down to the grotto that afternoon, to see the actual spring that Bernadette dug and the niche where the "beautiful lady" stood. She led us in her full Malta dress regalia, black cape with flashing red trim.

Malades accompanied by the Order of Malta are treated like royalty everywhere in Lourdes. When we arrived at the grotto, we found ourselves facing a hundred-yard-long line of pilgrims: ordinary tourists, sick pilgrims on their own, Knights and Dames of the Order of Malta waiting without malades. Kim said, "Follow me," and began walking with her usual complete assurance. About ten yards from the entrance to the cave, there was an opening in the fence that was holding back the tremendous line of people waiting in the fiendish sun, all of whom we had just waltzed past. She whipped her cape around and ushered us through this open gate, with barely an "excuse me" to the people behind us. They stepped back without protest—in fact, with broad smiles on their faces. The gate seemed to exist for exactly this reason.

I took Oscar out of his stroller and held him in front of me, facing outward. He was quiet, but as we advanced, he started bouncing up and down and waving his arms, cooing, "Ooooh! Ooooh!" His therapists had admonished us, twice a week without fail, to discourage him from "flapping," this thing he was now doing with special alacrity. I tried to hold his hands, but he kept bouncing and flapping. After a few more steps, we reached the wall of the cave, Oscar still flapping. He slapped both hands down on the cool rock, smoothed by millions of pilgrim hands, and instantly his entire body relaxed. His voice hushed. He froze as if he were hypnotized, his tiny, pudgy fingers caressing the wall so intently that the movement was almost imperceptible.

He melted.

I nudged Todd, walking next to me, who looked at Oscar and smiled. "He just went still," I murmured. "He's so calm."

The cave is a deep semicircular cavity in the face of the rock, and the line of people proceeds from left to right in slow, shuffling steps. A few more paces brought us to piles of fresh flowers and cards cast upon the ground before a clear glass wall. Behind the wall, the spring that Bernadette had dug still flowed freely, lit intentionally to look as if it were glowing from within.

Oscar continued to stare, his eyes round and wide, his body quiet but his face alert. The walk through the cave is a continuous path, but the face of the rock wall is not. Each time we took his hands away to move right, he began bouncing, flapping, and cooing again. Each time his hands touched a new part of the wall, he stilled as if he were listening to something. He was quiet, but it was not the kind of quiet we had gotten used to from him, oblivious to his surroundings. His was the quiet of a child absorbed in deep thought, trying to figure out some truth about the universe that is almost within his grasp.

We reached the deepest corner of the cave, mossy and moist. Water dripped from the ceiling and flowed silently down the walls. I leaned Oscar's head far back into the crevice to catch a few drops of the cold, clear water. They landed on his brow, and I rubbed them in. Throughout our slow walk, time had rearranged itself, and the crowds receded. The interior cocooned us, cool, dim, and hushed despite the throng of people. I felt we three were alone, and yet not alone, either. I experienced a palpable sense of being surrounded with motherly love and perfect care. Holiness dripped from the ceiling. We stepped lightly and freely among its puddles.

Along the outer edge of the cave on the opposite side, we stood directly beneath the niche that held the statue of Our Lady of Lourdes, where she first appeared to Bernadette. Oscar kept reaching out with both hands (even both legs!), and I let him touch the wall as much as he wanted. Even at our slow, ambling pace, we eventually reached the end of the cave. I folded Oscar's hands to his chest and stepped out onto the paved exit walkway with a pining regret.

Oscar began to protest—loudly. As we stepped onto the path he fussed, and by the time we were halfway down the walkway he was shrieking and arching his back, leaning back toward the grotto. The change was as sudden and astonishing as the peaceful change at the beginning had been.

"What's the matter?" Todd asked worriedly.

"I don't know!" I cried. "I can barely hold on to him, he's thrashing around so much. I think . . . I think he wants to go back."

Oscar had spent nearly a year working with a speech therapist back home. Most of their time together was spent on feeding therapy, teaching him to swallow and suck and chew, all the nearly invisible, instinctual movements that 99 percent of the world takes for granted. The therapist had only recently begun to introduce the rudiments of communication to Oscar. Each week, twice a week, hour upon hour, she encouraged him to express his preference in any available way—always subtle, always tiny, a hand movement that might have been accidental, a glance of the eye that lasted a split second longer than usual. She would take any hint of intentionality and run full speed with it: "Oh, you chose milk! Here's your milk." We were helping his brain to connect cause and effect, statement and outcome. It was arduous work, and the payoffs so far had been very limited. We celebrated with great exultation any sign, however slight and negligible, that Oscar understood that he could exert control over his little corner of the world.

Today, with his whole body (and considerable weight), in his fullest voice, Oscar was exerting that control. He was shouting at us to take him back there, put him back in that place, bring him back to his Mother. The intent was unmistakable. Todd, Oscar, and I were all in tears by the time we reached the end of the walkway, where the Dame had bathed his brow so tenderly during the grotto Mass. Oscar registered the holiness of that place, the presence of our Blessed Mother. That was what he had been listening for, the order of the universe he was trying to figure out. He knew her. He knew she was there.

He kept screaming with fury, throwing his hands up over his head, back in the direction of the grotto. "He wants to go back. Todd! Do you see this? Do you see how much he loves this place? I have never seen him be so clear about anything in his life."

Todd, eyes damp, leaned over and kissed the top of Oscar's head. "I know, buddy. Me too. I feel her too."

Oscar grasped Mary's presence there in a way few people probably can; he was mostly a creature of sense and emotion, not blocked and tempered by reason. I went to the grotto expecting a pleasant, banal springtime stroll and came out absolutely certain, for the first time since our slow-motion train wreck began a year before, that we are all loved completely, with a love beyond all measure. The child who (so far) could not be taught to communicate had communed with divine love, communed so fully and deeply that it shot out of him like lightning, like a sword piercing our hearts.

Before dinner that night, a volunteer invited me to write a prayer intention on a slip of paper. "We're doing a balloon release with all the child malades, with all their intentions, and we want Oscar to be included," she explained. I felt like so many prayers had been answered already. The fact remained, though, that our one prayer had not been answered, at least not yet. Oscar had not been healed. I felt strangely uncompelled to ask for that anymore, though. I mulled over my options for a while, at a loss now that my heart's single desire no longer seemed to be the thing I desired. I settled on an intention for the entire family, inspired by Todd's story of his time in the baths:

For healing for all of us
For peace
For the joy of God in our hearts

As we waited, I talked with other child malades I hadn't met: a diver who had been bound for the Olympics until he was paralyzed in a rollover crash, the parents of a boy with cystic fibrosis and only months to live. I realized I had barely scratched the surface of the amount of suffering right here on this pilgrimage—out of so many malades who had traveled on the same plane with us, I had met only a handful, and each of these carried an incomprehensible weight. There seemed no outer limit to the number of people carrying hidden burdens around, alone. My own suffering, Oscar's suffering, had seemed so immense when it was the only thing I could see; in the context of Lourdes, it was ordinary, even trivial. At the same time, I didn't feel dismissed or belittled, as I sometimes had when people tried to downplay or ignore our burdens at home. No one did that here. Our situation had become relegated to "ordinary" simply because we were all in this one big mess of a wonderful life together.

As we talked, we all fastened our intentions to the ribbon strings of our balloons. After the chaplain said a brief prayer, the children released their balloons together, and they hung overhead as bright red bubbles for a few moments before slipping off into the blue. Oscar had fallen asleep in his stroller, his balloon tied lightly around his ankle. When Matthias saw that it hadn't flown up yet, he ran over, gently loosened the slip knot, and lifted our family's prayers skyward for us. Immediately upon finishing this task, he began running around from one adult to the next, hugging each one and laughing brightly. I couldn't believe this was the same child Elizabeth had been describing earlier. I couldn't believe how love had remade his heart, and my own.

At dinner, everyone was out of uniform and dressed to the nines for the Farewell Program that evening. It leveled the playing field, erasing the lines between malades and volunteers. Just as Chase and Megan had stepped across to pray over us and serve us that afternoon, our pod members, who had been so professional and so focused on caring for us all week, began to open up more about their own lives. We weren't attending the next event on the pilgrimage schedule; we were just hanging out and eating with our family.

Oscar sat nearby in his stroller, kicking and chatting, lively as he had been all day. As he grew increasingly rowdy, Ryan asked, "Can I hold him? I need to get in as much Oscar time as I can before we go home."

I hated the sobering reminder that this paradise of mutual love and support would not last forever. Swallowing that thought, I

unbuckled Oscar and handed him to Ryan. "He's hungry. Why don't
you feed him?" I reached down and passed the formula to Ryan, who
settled Oscar in the crook of his knee like the seasoned father he was.

He made cutesy small talk with Oscar while he ate. "Hey, buddy!
Chow time! Wanna lie down and relax?" Eventually, they settled into
companionable silence, as Ryan just gazed down at him and Oscar
sucked, eyes gradually drooping as his pace slowed. "I love this kid. I
miss my own babies! My arms have felt empty all week. But I just love
this guy. There is something about him."

"Well, I have a crazy story," Amy offered. "I went to the baths this
morning."

"Ooh! Tell us about it!" everyone encouraged at once.

"I knew a lot about what to expect after our conversation the
other day. I knew the mechanics of what would happen. The weird
part happened after my bath, though.

"When I went in, I felt like I didn't really have anything I needed
to pray for, personally. So I decided to offer my bath for someone who
did need those graces—look at all the people I've met just this week. I
came here to serve, so this felt like another act of service. I told God,
'Whatever you had planned for me here today, just pass it on.'

"I've heard so much from everyone about how you dry off immediately. That didn't happen when they wrapped me back in the towel,
so I thought, 'Okay, maybe it happens as you get dressed.'

"I had all these layers of my uniform to put on, so I started with
my shirt, but I was still soaking wet. I mean, I was dripping all over the
floor. I thought, 'Huh, that's funny,' and kept going. I put on my skirt,
and my cardigan. Nope, still dripping. Cape and veil, still dripping.
Finally it was time to put on my hose and my shoes, and I thought
to myself, 'There are going to be puddles in my shoes! Why am I not
dry yet?'

"And then I heard a voice say, '*You told me I could pass it on.*'"

Everyone guffawed.

Amy laughed out loud, the victory of her punchline evident in
her glee. "I know! I couldn't believe it! God had to literally whack
me upside the head to make sure he had my attention. He passed my
graces on to someone else. Message received, loud and clear."

Next door after dinner, all four hundred of us crowded into the dining room for the farewell ceremony. Three pilgrims had been asked to give reflections, and they all spoke about variations on the same theme: how their prayers had been answered this week, in unexpected and elegant ways. God's designs are always more than ours—more challenging, more sacrificial, but far, far more loving. Travis, the paraplegic man who sat next to Todd and Oscar at the Mass of Healing, talked about how he hadn't even wanted to apply. He felt he had a good life and didn't need healing. After his experience here in Lourdes, though, he knew that God was calling him to move on to something more.

Elizabeth spoke next about the burnout of being a caregiving parent and how the patient, unwavering, single-minded care her family had received at Lourdes had taught her to surrender, while also alleviating some of the helplessness—and hopelessness—she felt in carrying these crosses at home alone. "They're pretty close to godparents, so we've decided to call them podparents," she quipped, to uproarious laughter and applause.

She finished on a more serious note, echoing what she had shared in our reflection group earlier that day: "This week was a foretaste of how God sees my kids, and who they will be with him in heaven. Our Lady of Lourdes was Jesus' caregiver. She is my children's caregiver and my caregiver and your caregiver.

"Even though we are leaving Lourdes, she will always be with us."

The final reflection was from Logan, the former diving star I had met that afternoon. He thanked his pod and the pilgrimage organizers, but mostly he thanked his mother, for never giving up on him, for pushing and loving and taking care of him since his injury. As he spoke about her devotion and courage, it felt like I was shedding layer after layer of dragon skin, all the self-protective whininess I had built up around myself about how I was too weak to do this, too sad to try, too burned out to keep going.

"I love you, Mom," he choked out through his tears. "Thank you for never giving up on me and never letting me give up either."

Instantly, ferociously, I wanted to be that for Oscar, even knowing that he would probably never be able to say words like that to me. I wanted to love him like Logan's mother loved Logan, like Our Lady of Lourdes loved me. I was ready to have my newfound heart torn open and poured out for him. I wanted again—and I had not wanted this in months—to bless his mission in this world, whatever it would be, with my grace-filled face.

22.

THE OTHER BRINK

"I can't believe this is it and that we're just going home to our regular lives. Everything has changed," I said moodily, as I stood with Todd and Carole before a long row of charter buses. *How could I carry this change back? What if I wasn't strong enough to sustain it?*

"It has changed. I've seen you this week, and *you* have changed. You are going to be fine. And you will always, always have us. The Order is your family now," Carole reassured me.

I nodded, feeling a bit lighter. "Those stories last night at the closing—the testimonies—were just amazing."

"It's an amazing place," she agreed. "This is my nineteenth pilgrimage, and every year it's just as amazing."

"How's little Oscar doing?" Another Dame leaned over his stroller, grabbing his toe to wiggle a hello.

"He's great," Todd answered simply. "He has been really alert and happy the last few days."

After the Dame strolled away, Carole grew thoughtful. "That's my friend Ruth. She is such a cheerful, positive person, you'd never know she's suffered some terrible losses. Her husband and her sister both died this year, but she never misses a pilgrimage."

"Wow," I breathed. Telling stories about people was one of Carole's favorite pastimes. She wasn't gossipy; rather, she passed things on as the Keeper of the Stories. She collected people, learned them, remembered them, and passed them on.

"There's another Dame here who brought her husband as a malade a few years ago. He had very advanced cancer, so sick he almost wasn't able to come, and he actually died during the pilgrimage," she went on.

"What?" Todd and I said in shock, nearly in unison.

"She finished the pilgrimage anyway. I remember how beautiful that was. We offered to send them home, of course, but she wanted to continue. I think it ended up being very comforting for her. She felt like he had the most peaceful death possible," Carole continued, almost as if we hadn't spoken. "The thing about Lourdes is that everyone is suffering. But the volunteers come anyway. Sometimes they're here exactly because of it." She fixed me with an unwavering gaze at that last line.

The subtext reverberated loud and clear. I had seen it all along, all week. Life was possible after a horrible, painful twist of fate, perhaps even more so when that pain was offered as a gift to others in need. The trick now, Carole was implying, was to live that out.

I drank in a last, wistful look at the river, the picturesque hotels with their crooked roofs, the rough mountaintops, these places my heart now cherished so deeply. Even the paving stones made me sentimental; I wondered when I would ever see them again. My heart bordered on breaking from the weight of the goodbye, so I resolved instead to say so long. I had to come back, somehow, because the alternative was unendurable. I could not live the rest of my life without seeing this place again.

At the airport, I finally put a finger on something that had been niggling at the back of my mind all week. "This might be a weird question," I began, "but I get the sense that you're not supposed to ask what's wrong with the malades. Is that true?"

Kim and Carole glanced at each other briefly, then nodded.

"So none of you actually have any idea what's wrong with Oscar?" I asked, puzzling out the logical conclusion that had been staring me in the face for days.

"No, no one who isn't on the medical team," Carole confirmed.

There was a long pause, and then she finally broke into a grin. "So, what's wrong with him?"

The podparents had shared enough by this point that it was a perfectly natural question, not a violation of a sacred boundary. We were friends, even family, and they had a right to know. Dispassionately at first, I began to recount Oscar's illness from the day of his first seizure, that night he awoke shaking in my arms, and how the Dominican sisters prayed us all the way to the hospital. ·

As I talked, the team's faces began to soften with that pity I had grown to hate so much, and at first I stiffened, growing clipped and clinical. With a second look, though, I discerned that it wasn't pity. This was compassion, in the literal sense, *com-passio*, a "suffering with." They had grown to love this boy, and the telling of this story caused them to suffer along with us.

Still, there was a lot to tell. I made it as brief as I could. I hadn't told the story in a long time, and I noticed that I was able to tell it without having to detach my emotions entirely, without recounting medical information like a robotic nurse. I could observe it from a distance, invite the memories of those moments into my heart, and even relive the feelings. The telling of my son's past did not break me.

"Where were you?" I thought back to the words I had screamed at Jesus after every painful encounter. "Where were you?" I whispered again, testing, searching.

"I was here," he answered, as he described the Dominican sisters praying for us as we raced down darkened streets to the hospital. "And here," my mother sitting at my side until my husband arrived, as worried as I was but strong for me. "And here," the nurse bringing me a cup of freshly brewed coffee at 4 a.m. "And here," a card that had arrived in the mail, announcing a novena of Masses being said in honor of our family. "And here," a holy medal someone had touched to a relic of St. Nicholas, whose feast day was Oscar's birthday, before she pressed it into my hand.

"And here, and here. I was here."

I finished the litany of troubles, the litany of answers I had never heard. *I will be with you, and I will help you.* We all looked at each other. Nothing I had said was any worse than anything they had heard before, or seen before, or even lived out this very week.

"I'm so sorry for everything you've been through, but it has been an honor to be here with you," Kim finally put in.

"I can't say I'm glad it all happened, but this pilgrimage has been a gift. A lot of things have been fixed that I didn't know needed fixing. I can see already how God has brought good out of it, and I never, ever thought I'd be able to say that," I admitted quietly.

"Why don't we all grab some lunch and sit down?" Everyone took one of the brown bags the Order had provided. When we found some seats, Carole and Kim insisted that Oscar be allowed to sit on the bench between them. They cooed and fussed over him like two grandmothers, and Todd and I took a moment by ourselves to eat.

As we moved down the row a few seats, we passed another Dame wearing a badge whose name I recognized: Betty. At the beginning of the week, along with our schedules and directories and room keys, the Order had distributed a small card to each of us bearing the name of a fellow pilgrim. This person, the card explained, was our prayer partner; our job was to keep them in our hearts as we went from event to event, offering prayers for the success of their pilgrimage. I had only seen one card, so I assumed that Todd and I were a "package deal," that we should pray for Betty together and someone else would pray for us as a couple.

We set our lunches down, and I whispered to Todd, "Let's go introduce ourselves!" He nodded and followed me.

"Excuse me?" I tapped the woman on the shoulder. "I'm Christy Wilkens, and this is Todd—we're baby Oscar's parents." That phrase was now our standard Lourdes introduction. Baby Oscar was a celebrity; we were the entourage. "I just wanted to let you know that we were your prayer partners this week. It was an honor to pray for you, and I hope you've had a good pilgrimage."

"Oh, nice to meet you!" Her eyes shone happily. "Thank you; yes, it's been wonderful."

As we made our way back to the seats, Todd leaned over and whispered in my ear. "You know, she was your prayer partner. I had a different one."

"You did? Why didn't you tell me? I only ever saw one card, and I kept making you pray for her with me!" I laughed. "Who was yours?"

He looked at me out of the corner of his eyes.

"You were."

How could I leave? How could I go home and face my life without all this help? It was like being informed that it was time for me to be buried alive again.

Despite my early wakeup, sleep eluded me completely on the flight home. Oscar and Todd napped, but I just couldn't. The party atmosphere on the plane did not help me feel any sleepier. On the outbound flight, it had been mostly the volunteers who were chatty and loose. Now, everyone onboard was full of life.

I did my best to find an outlet for my nervous energy. I scribbled notes in my journal. I exchanged pleasantries with Vito, sitting just ahead of me like the last time. Ryan and I traded seats so I could admire Kim's needlework and learn about her technique. I wished I had brought something to do with my hands too. Beneath the surface, my tension and sadness mounted with every westbound mile. I wasn't sure I could manage letting our life raft go.

When we landed at JFK, there was no organized farewell, no songs or trumpets, just people gathering their bags and wandering off. Our pilgrimage was breaking apart, rivulets running away in every direction, diverted into new streams. The goodbyes came quickly and erratically, in the midst of chaos and distraction. Carole had to grab a taxi crosstown for her connecting flight out of a different airport; after a brief and harried hug, she ran, and she was gone. Ryan collected his bags, gave each one of us a solid squeeze, rubbed his giant hand over Oscar's hair one last time, and stepped out into the crowded airport.

Megan and Chase had found us in the crowd, but I hadn't seen Joyce, or Steve, or Elizabeth, or . . . so many people! Megan

held Oscar for a long time, while we searched for our luggage. He
was downright rowdy now, smiling and chatting with abandon,
smacking his hands down on her chest in glee. Chase handed us a
plaid blanket sporting the trademark red, black, and white of the
Order of Malta. "We figured you could use it in the airport so that
Oscar has a place to play on the floor." I was nearly undone by the
kindness of this small but thoughtful gesture, one of thousands I
had experienced this week as a matter of course. Would we ever
again be taken care of with such lavish and gratuitous love?

We exchanged phone numbers and hugs, and then Chase and
Megan walked away. Kim helped us find our stroller, hugged us,
and walked away. We took our own luggage and stepped away from
the crowd uncertainly.

Was that really it? Just walk away?

Amy found us at that moment with her own luggage, and we
fell upon her, glad for even a momentary reprieve. Ten minutes
later, we had all cleared customs, and Amy's gate was one way, ours
another. We hugged. She walked away. Every other pilgrim, every
face we had known and come to love, had receded into the crowded
terminals, lost inside the endless, impersonal sea of passengers.

Oscar needed a clean diaper, but we had used every one we'd
packed; I spent $17 on two diapers and some Dramamine. We
ordered noodles, after watching the server loudly berate the guy
in front of us for standing in the middle of the counter instead of
directly under the "order here" sign. The overripe trash cans, the
garbled overhead announcements, the brash, sickening lighting—
all of it overwhelmed my newly rewired sensibilities. Welcome
back to America.

Todd and I sat at a two-top table, poking at our noodles, while
Oscar slept next to us in heedless content. I felt strangely discon-
nected from Todd, too, as if the severing of pilgrimage bonds
had accidentally severed one too many. We didn't say much, both
exhausted, shy with each other now that we were alone again,
without a safety net of communal love to prop up our neophyte
attempts at the marital kind. We fell back on old habits, on silence
and logistics, but when he reached across the table for my hand

midway through our meal, I reached back. I met his eyes. We smiled, weakly. It was something.

None of these people in the airport had any idea what had just happened to us. We had experienced more upheaval in a week than some people experience their entire lives, and diapers were still being sold for outrageous margins and noodle-shop ladies were still yelling at customers like nothing had changed.

Didn't they know? How could they not know that everything had changed?

23.

What I Have Seen and Heard

My parents had kept the kids one last night, so we could get a final precious night's sleep before the onslaught; they all came roaring in the door the next morning. We hugged and kissed and cried and laughed. Everyone was overjoyed to see Oscar, who had always reigned as king of the household, uncontested in popularity and adorableness.

Amid their clamoring for presents, I was surprised that no child thought to ask whether Oscar had been healed, especially not the ones who were still young enough to think it was a totally reasonable thing to expect miracles. We are a story-driven household, and all of these little ones lived and breathed fairy tales and Bible stories, steeped in good-versus-evil melodrama and *deus ex machina* endings. Princesses were rescued from dragons as a matter of course, and Jesus fed thousands with five loaves and two fish just by opening his mouth to say so.

Our five-year-old son, Benny, had asked during a phone call while we were still in France: "Mama, is Oscar still sick?" He had asked in the same way an adult might ask a coworker in passing: "Hey, how's your cold?" I had hedged against his innocent blind faith. "He's doing really well and we're having a wonderful time. I can't wait for you to see him again!" After our return home, though, no one asked, not even that curious, trusting child. I was grateful for the reprieve. I wasn't sure I was ready to deal with the crisis of faith that might ensue if we had to tell them, no, he wasn't. He still had seizures. He still needed medicine. He still couldn't walk or talk.

They were too busy simply smothering him with kisses, rejoicing in having their good old, familiar, sick Oscar back home. When the time came to leave for therapy—no rest for the weary—there were tears and wailing and gnashing of teeth, and I had to pry him out of the arms of a very unwilling sister, who was delighted to have her living baby doll back.

His twice-weekly physical therapy had been like therapy for me too. We had worked with the same therapist, Carole, for more than a year, starting only weeks after his seizures began. She was tough, funny, and supremely confident in her (admittedly stellar) skills; for every question about Oscar's condition, she had an answer or knew who to ask for one. We had spent an inordinate number of intimate hours together, Carole and I, and she had seen both the best and the worst of me. She had never once coddled me, never pacified me with an easy, untrue answer. Her honesty and her love were both unyielding.

As Carole worked with Oscar that first day back, I fumbled through a tired and confused retelling of our trip, trying to envelop what had happened in a patched-up pile of raggedy words. To my own ears, I sounded like the five kids I had left back at home, recounting the minutiae of their days in extended detail. "And then we went for a walk, and we saw a *red bug*!" my children would exclaim.

"And then we walked to Mass with funny blue carts and there was a *cardinal*," I tried gamely.

As I talked, Carole smiled up at me occasionally. "You look good, hon. You look relaxed. It's good to see you smiling again." She was distracted, though. Ordinarily, she maneuvered Oscar's body into various positions with professional efficiency, multitasking while we chatted the entire hour. When Oscar would buck his torso backward without warning or throw his arms and legs out spastically, she would focus her attention on him briefly, without ever losing her train of thought.

This day, though, she interrupted me at several points. "He's very *calm*." I nodded and went on with my story. She wasn't looking at me; she was looking at him, her head cocked to one side. "No, I mean his body is very *organized*." As I continued talking, I watched how she worked, and I watched how Oscar responded. He wasn't bucking or kicking. He just moved quietly, cooperatively. It looked like a dance instead of a wrestling match.

I kept trying to convey the gravity and enormity of everything that had happened to us, with heightened drama and fervor, and she kept ignoring me and studying my child. She chimed in with an occasional "Uh-huh," but her eyes were locked on Oscar, eyebrows furrowed in puzzlement.

As I was packing our bags to leave, Carole told me, "Christy, he's completely different. Completely."

"What do you mean?" I asked cautiously. I continued methodically replacing baby wipes, chew toys, and socks into the diaper bag, without raising my eyes.

"He's peaceful, and calm, and so much more alert. I gotta tell you . . . I'm a little freaked out."

Nothing that I could recall had ever freaked Carole out. No news, no matter how devastating or unusual. Carole was unfreakable.

On the way home, I chatted with Todd about it over speakerphone. "Maybe he's . . . actually better. Are we not just imagining this? I think other people can see it too."

"Absolutely, he's better. There's not a doubt in my mind. Our son was healed," Todd stated, openly and unreservedly. There it was, the best of my husband's faith on full display: sincerity and practicality. He refused to hedge or second-guess but accepted Oscar's gift at face value. He had always accepted the gift of Oscar at face value.

A few days later, Oscar and I visited his neurologist. Oscar had seen the same neurologist, Dr. Keough, every few weeks since the night of his very first seizure. She had covered every EEG and hospital stay, reviewing countless hours of video footage. She knew Oscar as intimately as any physician could, from his quirky electrical brainwaves to his floppy, unstable ankles.

As soon as she walked into the room, she greeted me, then him. "Wow, he's really alert! Hi, Oscar!"

He looked up at her serenely and surely.

"Hi, buddy! I'm impressed that he responded to his name. That's new, isn't it?" This last part was directed to me. "He looks great! How was your trip?"

Again, I launched into a recounting of the trip, a little better rehearsed and a little less jet-lagged this time. Oscar was watching Dr. Keough closely. I moved him from his stroller to the exam table, and she burst out, "Wow!"

This was not a woman given to *wow*.

"He didn't used to sit up so straight. Look at his back!"

One side effect of both Oscar's neurological issues and his medications is low muscle tone. He had, until last week, been a slouchy boy, completely folding himself in half like a rag doll when he grew weary. "He's been sitting up ramrod straight like that since we came home," I answered. "He's not losing his balance and falling over, like he used to, or throwing his torso backward and arching."

Dr. Keough looked at him and smiled, saying, "Oscar, you're sitting up like such a big boy! Yay!" She clapped her hands in delight.

He looked her dead in the eye, smiled back, and moved his hands together three times.

She and I looked at each other in total and mutual shock.

"He's clapping," I choked.

"I think he did," she said. "Yay!" She leaned over him again and repeated her clapping, this time with even more enthusiasm. He smiled back and did it again.

Dr. Keough looked at me, wonder in her eyes. "Have you ever seen this before?"

The following Saturday, Todd was driving our family home in the van. May in Texas is hot, and that day was no exception. Our passenger crew was uniformly tired and a wee bit cranky, the kind of cranky that leads one child to provoke a fight by invading her brother's personal space by two inches, and another child to passive-aggressively request a song that he knows his sister loathes.

Oscar may be nonverbal, but he has never been nonemotional, and he sensed the tension in the van, our canary in the coal mine. He began to whimper, then to fuss, then to just plain cry. The only choice now was to amuse Oscar in the hopes of avoiding a full-scale meltdown, because they tended to be contagious.

I talked and sang silly songs, and he began to cheer up by degrees, watching me, but still sober as a judge. Every time I stopped, even briefly, Oscar picked right up fussing where he had left off. After ten minutes or so, I grew weary of "Pat-a-Cake" and ran out of verses of "Wheels on the Bus," even the made-up ones. (*The dogs on the bus go arf, arf, arf . . .*) In desperation, I covered my face with my hands, then popped out and cried, "Peekaboo!"

I was truly out of ideas. Peekaboo had never once worked in over a year of trying.

Todd and I had tried it. Oscar's siblings had all tried it. His many therapists had tried it, even using animatronic talking teddy bears to spice things up. The best you could hope for was a moment's eye contact and maybe a brief smile, but Oscar just didn't get it. When he smiled, he was responding to your smile, not to the sense of anticipation or to the joke of the sudden reveal. Usually, he would only look once or twice—and then only if you were particularly passionate in your delivery—before tuning out in his usual hazy daze.

This time, he looked at me from the corner of his eye and smiled when I uncovered my face. Grasping eagerly at straws, I tried it again, covering my own face, then reappearing with a grossly exaggerated expression and abnormally loud "Peekaboo!" His smile grew wider, and he turned his head to face me. I doggedly repeated myself, and after a few more rounds, he was still watching, sucking hard on his pacifier. His grin split open, and he rewarded me with a small giggle.

Giggles from Oscar were hard to come by, and we had shattered all previous peekaboo records. Not wanting to break the spell, I didn't stop to call anyone else's attention to what was happening. I leaned over, and this time I covered his face instead of mine. When I moved my hands away with a "Boo!" he squealed with delight, spit out his pacifier, and laughed out loud.

The next time I covered his face, he raised his own hand and placed it on top of mine. When I moved, he moved, and when I booed, he chortled with glee.

We played peekaboo the rest of the way home. By the end, each time I covered his face, he pushed my arm down himself, howling with laughter before I even rewarded him with the big monkey-faced payoff. "Peekaboo!"

He totally got the joke. It was the first joke he ever understood.

I can't explain, from today's vantage point, how I didn't accept these remarkable things for the marvels that they were, right away. Certainly, after so many failed therapies and medication trials, I had learned to guard my heart and second-guess any sign of improvement, always waiting for the other shoe to drop because experience had proven that it always would. Perhaps I had been too blindsided by my experience in the baths, the wallowing darkness I had embraced that night, the certainty that no miracle was coming.

Still, how could I have failed to notice that Oscar was easily accomplishing things that his therapists had pleaded with him to do for months without success, starting the very day after those horrible baths? He had pulled up to his knees in the voiture during the eucharistic procession, thrown his toys around like an unruly (and neurotypical) toddler. He had smiled brightly at his godparents when they arrived, cooing and waving with excitement at their familiar faces. He had displayed unmistakable, unrestrained grief when we walked out of Mary's grotto. He had babbled, in turns and on video, with Kim in our hotel room one afternoon, when he had never babbled or taken turns at anything before.

Our Austin community—family, friends, clergy, teachers, doctors, therapists—all knew we had taken a trip and why we had gone, but I never mentioned anything about the changes in Oscar when we returned. I didn't need to. Every person who knew him well did not fail to comment with wonder upon the differences.

The astonishment of our community, one person after the next, startled me out of my own complacency. My eyes were opened, my heart awakened, and I started to see the remarkable things for what they were.

Todd talks to process his thoughts; I write. After several blog posts about our Lourdes pilgrimage, the story of our experience crystallized in my mind. I made connections, saw signs, noticed themes that I hadn't noticed at the time. The more I wrote, the surer I became.

We had, all three of us, been granted miracles on that pilgrimage—miracles, plural.

The spring liturgical seasons took on an intensely personal meaning. I had lived Good Friday intimately, through an entire year of agony that had shaken the foundations of my faith like an earthquake and rent the temple veil in two. In Lourdes, we had lived Easter, our old lives buried and glorious new ones resurrected in their place.

But the time after Easter was both ecstatic and disorienting, for me as it must have been for the first apostles. It demanded a completely altered worldview. Everything I thought I knew was wrong; impossible things happened every day before breakfast. After Jesus conquered death, he appeared to his disciples over the next forty days, always in his glorified, still-wounded body—and they weren't usually quick to recognize him. Every time, Jesus performed a physical, tangible miracle, and then their eyes were opened. And every time, after the fact, the disciples asked themselves, "How could we not have seen it?" I wondered the same of myself, of our glory, and of our wounds.

On Pentecost, the birthday of the Church and the day the Holy Spirit empowered the disciples to preach Christ's gospel to the world, I adopted in earnest the words of St. Bernadette from her family's little cachot: *I am entrusted with telling you what I have seen and heard.* That day, I published a piece outlining Oscar's amazing progress in painstaking detail, honoring my promise, unapologetically hurling the word "miracle" forth from my mouth into the world. By the end of the week, the article had been read and shared thousands of times. Even if I wasn't entrusted with making people believe it . . . they did.

24.

RISE, TAKE UP YOUR MAT

A few weeks later, while tidying up and prepping dinner, the hymn "It Is Well with My Soul" popped up on my Spotify playlist.

This song had been my anthem during my Year of Despair. If there was anything I did right during those months (as opposed to the many, many things I'm quite sure I did wrong), it was to hold on to the possibility, however faint and nonsensical, that God could redeem the Greek tragedy that our lives had become: a child's devastating diagnosis, our failing marriage, my near apostasy. The story of the hymn, composed by a man who lost his livelihood in a fire and his family in a shipwreck only weeks apart, is itself a Greek tragedy.

This song had been playing during the retreat with my friends when I had publicly crumbled beneath the weight of my sorrow, when they desperately, heroically tried to climb down into my darkness and walk me through it, their only armament the light of love.

This song had been playing when, despite my friends' valiant efforts, my heart of stone—the impervious wall I had built between myself and God, pebble by furious pebble—had shattered into a million unfixable splinters, a puzzle whose jagged pieces I could never hope to reassemble.

This song had rung in my ears during the many wretched, repeated moments when I gave up even pretending to try to believe in a God who loved me or cared about Oscar.

I stopped to listen now, dishrag in hand. I realized that she was gone: the mother hemorrhaging the lifeblood of her faith, the paralytic

who refused to be lowered, the blind man who said "no thanks" to
the dirt-and-spit mud, that messy grace of Jesus' mercy. Whatever
had happened to the recipients of these biblical miracles before they
encountered Jesus, it only took one split second to be overturned.
For every moment I had given up, I had gotten up and turned back
to God just once more.

God blesses our faithfulness, however weak. God drew forth
beautiful goodness from rubble and ashes, refashioned my splintered
heart from the dust.

I had felt like a hypocrite as I prepared for Lourdes. I had under-
taken the pilgrimage almost out of spite, one final opportunity to dis-
prove the existence and perfection of God. I thought physical healing
for Oscar was impossible, spiritual healing for me equally impossible.
When we left the baths that Friday in Lourdes, my dejection was
complete. Oscar was the same, and I did not feel any better. The pilgrimage was for nothing.

But a pilgrimage is a surrender: not an abstract idea, but a movement of the heart and body. Flying across the world was a physical
act. Allowing strangers to feed, shelter, and anoint our family was a
physical act. Placing my son in someone else's arms was a physical
act. What I needed in that moment in the baths at Lourdes was to
surrender Oscar to God, physically. Giving ourselves up to the waters
was the ultimate act of submission. I released his body. I released
my own. I laid down every single thing I had been using as a shield
between me and God.

I traded control for vulnerability.

I didn't ask for a miracle because I believed. I asked because I
was desperate and angry, like the pilgrim whose dialysis machine had
failed. I knew there was absolutely nothing else I could do, say, try, or
pray . . . and I thought that was the end of the story.

But into that unguarded emptiness, in the dark night, God moved.
The powerlessness and despair I felt after the baths were absolutely
true and absolutely necessary, just as Lazarus had to die, and his family
had to endure an agony of suffering, so that God's glory could be more
fully revealed when Christ called his stinking, rotting body forth from
the tomb, live and fresh and whole.

I forgot that God blesses and multiplies our movements toward him, the tiny ones and the large ones alike, in unexpected and wildly generous ways. I forgot that this is the God who hung the stars. I forgot that if he could breathe life into chaotic nothingness, he could breathe life into my dry-bones, dust-and-ashes self. I forgot that he is in the waiting too.

By the end of the pilgrimage, God had put my soul back together, in proper order, in four days flat. That was my miracle.

And, like Amy's story in the baths, when she left dripping wet because God had answered her prayer and passed her promised graces on to someone else, he wanted to make sure I couldn't miss the fact that he had answered mine.

In fact, he had answered the one I hadn't even realized I had been praying, or that I had forgotten I had offered. I had promised God shortly after my children were born that I wanted to be totally his, to belong to him completely. I had even asked Mary, explicitly and repeatedly, for her help in achieving this goal, by consecrating myself into her protection and care each year.

God took me at my word, and he took my most precious possession. He took the health of my child. He asked me to sacrifice my son, as he had asked Abraham to sacrifice Isaac on the mountaintop, to be willing to trust him with his life . . . or his death. In doing so, he gave me back my life, fully belonging to him now. Even better, he used Mary to achieve that goal, just as I had asked.

Then he went ahead and healed my son, because he needed me to notice what he'd already done for me. Our friends in the Order of Malta had carried us to a place we could never have reached ourselves and lowered us through the roof. Moved by their faith, when my own was negligible, Jesus moved a mountain. The physical miracle pointed to the spiritual one that had already taken place. *We have seen remarkable things today.*

C. S. Lewis once asked the obvious question: Why did God need Abraham to sacrifice Isaac? An omniscient God must have known what Abraham would do; why make him do it? Lewis, paraphrasing St. Augustine, explains, "The obedience which he did not know he would choose, he cannot be said to have chosen. The reality of Abraham's obedience was the act itself."[1]

The obedience is the act. My obedience was to undertake the journey and to put my son in the water. Just as Abraham brought Isaac to the mountain, fully prepared to go through with the sacrifice until the crucial last split second when his hand was stayed and a ram was provided, a wink and a nod from God. Just as the four friends lowered the paralytic through the roof, and Christ forgave his sins and claimed him entirely as his own, healing his body as an afterthought and a signpost to others.

Oscar never needed to be healed, you see. Our number-one goal is to get our children to heaven, to return them to the Father who loaned them to us. Oscar is cognitively incapable of sin, even after Lourdes, possibly forever. As a baptized Christian in a perfect state of grace, he has a one-way ticket to heaven. God nudged a camel through the eye of a needle, healing Oscar enough to help my unbelief, without changing a single thing about him that would alter God's purpose or plan for his life. The cross, transformed from curse to blessing, would remain. That was Oscar's miracle.

Todd had known this all along. His security in that knowledge had been the seat of his deep peace about Oscar's situation, the peace that I had used to drive a wedge between us. Now I too was secure in the knowledge of our belovedness, secure with clear eyes and full breaths and restful sleep. That security allowed me to do something I hadn't done in a long time. I turned back to my husband, and we began to talk.

"I can't believe it," I remarked one exhausted evening. Todd and I sat on the couch, my legs wrapped over his, our hands entwined. "The pilgrimage seems like a dream now, or a fairytale. Sitting here in our living room, it doesn't seem like something that really happened to us. But I know how I felt sitting here in our living room two weeks ago, and I can't believe how much has changed."

"I know," he agreed. Todd hadn't been very open about his own struggles during that year of Oscar's illness. He would have, though. He would have been ready to talk about any of this, at any time, if I hadn't busily and relentlessly barred the door of my heart against him. For his part, he had grown weary of making effort after effort and being rebuffed time and again; I had taught him to stop trying to connect. My obstinacy and self-absorption had been poison sown at the roots of our relationship every day, until Todd, stymied, had abandoned his efforts to revive it. How close our marriage had come to oblivion!

I murmured, "It's so good that we got to go together. I don't think there's any possible way I could have explained to you what happened on that trip, if you hadn't been there with me."

"We both needed to go," he said. "We both needed to go for our own reasons, but we both needed to be there for Oscar too. It was important for our whole family. That's why I carried that petition into the baths. We all needed healing, not just Oscar."

"You're right." I rested my head on his chest, suffused with warmth. Gratitude. What wonders, to be sitting on the couch with my husband, connected and affirmed. For the first time in months, we had shared something together. We felt like a team again. The connection was sublime and ridiculously simple. How had this, just being in the same room together, been so hard for so long?

"Oscar's progress is a miracle," Todd said. "The way everyone else at home is responding to him is like seeing his healing all over again, with new eyes, every day. Thanks be to God." Todd peppered his days with that phrase, always out loud. It was one of the things I loved about him, his total willingness to lay praise and thanks at God's feet, all day, every day.

"Thanks be to God," I echoed, a little sleepily. Todd's Mary medal from the Bethlehem shop hung from his neck, and I stared at the corner that just peeked above his collar. He was never without it now— Todd's Lourdes miracle, recognizing his Mother. My senses took in the dim lamplight, my husband's heartbeat in my ear, the cicadas humming outside the window. For a moment, the veil between the worlds lifted at the corner, and I breathed in the peace of Lourdes—the peace that passes understanding, right here in my untidy living room. Mary was in the middle of our embrace.

"My heart is so tender. It's like Lourdes was a meat tenderizer," he joked, and I laughed, a genuine laugh. "I keep getting bowled over by things I never would have noticed before. And I see how lucky we are. Every minute I see again how God turned this horrible thing to good. It's so much better than what I imagined when we heard that we were going."

We were quiet then. This, our final miracle: two hearts of flesh, tender with the mercies of a new day, beating together on the couch.

25.

CHOSEN, BLESSED, BROKEN, GIVEN

Oscar enjoyed five solid months of good health. He did not experience a single seizure, nor anything worse than a runny nose. He continued to make steady forward progress in therapy sessions, chipping away at developmental milestones bit by bit, even if there were no more explosive overnight gains. No hospital stays, few specialist consults—we coasted long and far on the spectacular graces of the pilgrimage.

In early fall, though, I found myself sitting in Mass, surrounded by family and friends who love us and support us. Despite their support, I was in tears. My wound of loneliness—even of abandonment—had been eased but not erased by our pilgrimage. In Lourdes, I had been cradled by God in the hands of the people around me. Months later, the newfound trust that had felt so unshakable was being worn away by the daily grind, just as I had feared on our plane ride home.

Later that same week, Oscar got sick—*really* sick.

We took him to the ER for labs and fluids. I texted all of our kids' godparents, asking for prayers, and posted a quick update on Facebook. While I fretted, alarmed that no one understood why our son had been actively vomiting for twelve hours, the ER door slid open, and someone walked in carrying a huge box.

"Hi!" chirped Joan Whiteson. "I didn't know how long you would be here, but I thought you could use some provisions." Joan was an acquaintance from my parish. We were friendly, but not close, certainly not intimate enough that I would expect her to pop in during a bona fide medical emergency. She gave me a hug and began to unpack gourmet sandwiches and soups, fancy artisanal sodas—enough food for six people. "How's our boy doing?"

"Not great, honestly. But we're hanging in there. Thank you so much for coming! I . . . don't know what to say. This is such a surprise." I spoke warmly, hoping that she could not sense my confusion and introvert panic. How could I graciously host someone I didn't know very well in an ER exam room while my son was lying on the table puking?

"I saw your post, and I know how these things can go on and on. We live nearby. I wanted to make sure you had options other than the vending machine," she explained with a cheerful smile and a dismissive wave, as if showing up unannounced with epicurean delights were a completely ordinary thing to do. "These are all from my favorite little neighborhood cafe."

I was taken aback by her audacious move. In the same heartbeat, I realized I was famished, worried, and hungry for company. We sat and talked while I ate, and she held my hand while the nurses performed a gruesome catheterization on Oscar, painful enough to rouse him from his stupor and leave him howling in agony. I have no idea what we talked about, on hard plastic chairs under fluorescent lights amid the smell of soup and antiseptic. This absurd setting became the backdrop for what was one of maybe three conversations I had ever had with Joan. I was bewildered, but grateful.

A hospital stay is disorienting, an alternate reality. Hospital time bears no resemblance to regular time. Hospital food bears no resemblance to regular food. During most of our previous stays, I had talked to no one but immediate family and medical personnel for the duration. Then I had surfaced for air, cleared my head, and tried to resume my regular life, now a flaming wreckage of neglected appointments and duties.

But during this hospital visit, God used our community to bridge that unbridgeable gap, repeatedly, in the most surprising and unexpected ways.

Oscar was admitted to the hospital from the ER. Joan's box, it turned out, sustained me through several more meals, because that hospital admission would prove to be the longest of Oscar's life thus far. The shadow of death hovered at the edges of the room more than once before we solved the mystery: he was allergic to his formula. After retooling his entire diet from scratch, we were finally sent home.

In the meantime, during two hellish weeks, the steady stream of support kicked off by Joan continued unabated. Friends delivered dinners for Todd at home and took kids for playdates. The emergency department chief of medicine dropped by our room to personally check on Oscar's progress. A friend brought me Communion on Sunday and stayed for a visit, breaking up the monotonous hours of HGTV and Dr. Pepper. Another friend snuck in contraband cocktails after a long day mothering her own small children. Oscar's godfather, Peter, delivered an explosively colorful blanket to ward off the chill of the room and the relentlessly bland yellow of its walls.

The visit I treasured most was from someone I had never actually met before; we had been introduced via email because her teenaged son also suffered from epilepsy. She sat with me for hours, and we spoke the tough-but-tender secret language of parents who have seen and endured far too much of our children's pain. When I was too timid to raise an alarm about a possible seizure Oscar was having, she marched out and dragged in a nurse by the elbow.

Oscar's nurses commented at one point that I was remarkably calm and chipper; I shrugged and answered that clearly people must be praying their knees raw on our behalf. When the room wasn't filled with visitors, my text messages were buzzing off the hook. *When can we see you? What do you need? We offered Mass for you this morning, a Rosary, a chaplet.*

I had to laugh, and I had to shake my head. The temptations (to despair, to control, to fear) did not cease after our pilgrimage to Lourdes. If anything, the temptations increased. It's easy after "coming down the mountain" from a profound experience of God's love to fall back into old habits of not trusting. The empty wilderness beckons and the wild beasts prowl, seeking the ruin of souls. Just when I was quite certain that God wasn't listening and we had been abandoned to shoulder our miseries alone again, he showed up in the faces and hands of my friends. He showered us with his outlandish, unmistakable, foolish generosity, swathed in small, simple gifts to our family. The temptations set me up to be reminded of God's unfailing help through his ministering angels, who came bearing soup and blankets and a little tequila, bearing Jesus himself to my son's bedside.

Generous love on pilgrimage transformed our emotional suffering into a deep, abiding joy and confidence in God's mercy. It reminded us of our belovedness.

I discovered the same generous love in Austin too. The depth of people caring about our family was not a fluke that could only happen in an esoteric, highly spiritualized setting in mountainous France, removed from everyday cares. God had just proven that the same kind of overpowering, altruistic love—the love of a community working together in service—could happen here, in my regular life. That love had existed all along, and it still flourished. I had learned enough in Lourdes to say yes to every single offer, unashamedly. I recognized the need to let our community have their (local) pilgrimage, too, to serve Christ through serving us, with their hands and feet and not just their prayers.

Now that my own knees were no longer weak with fear and loneliness, I could see how simple this type of active love was in practice. Together with our local community, we had weathered our first setback since Lourdes. For too long, I had clung to the excuse that our crazy schedule and complicated needs precluded me from offering anything to others, forgetting that even Jesus had been crushed by his own impotence as he fell, again and again, on his way to Calvary. Yet just as Jesus allowed Simon to help him carry the cross, when I followed in his footsteps and allowed others to help me, I too was offering an act of love. And Jesus did not remain where he fell. He rose and took the next excruciating step, and the one after that, until he broke open the gates of heaven and restored the world for us.

This time, after *my* stumble, I too stood back up and kept walking, in more resolute and more communal ways. In the aftermath of our latest crisis, one friend or acquaintance after another faced their own mental, physical, or emotional crisis. No longer paralyzed, I took up my mat, my newly restored limbs now uniquely equipped to serve my friends, or simply to stand vigil in their personal darkness. I knew what to do, as if a powerful instinct had been awakened from deep slumber. I emailed and called. I mailed package after package of Lourdes water, sending prayers to cover each one. I delivered meals to hospital rooms. I stopped ignoring those small promptings of my heart. I stopped hiding under the cover of "I am suffering too much to help." I stepped across the line, as Chase and Megan had done for us that day in the *Chemin de Consolation*. We surrendered our wounds to each other, submitted our needs to another's care. The rising tide of merciful, active love lifts all boats.

What happens in Lourdes overturns our relentless societal habit of normalizing one set of bodies—one set of humans—over others. Sometimes illness and disability are characterized as solely belonging to the individual, who deviates from a "mean," falls off a "curve," or is located outside the "norm." More recent theories place the problem between the person and the environment, a problem of misfit and mismatch: a *social* problem.

Both models partly obscure what Jesus showed us in his miraculous healings, repeatedly: neither disability nor ability are entirely personal or entirely social. Neither is solely physical. The Lourdes conception of the "beloved malade" adjusts the frame. Lourdes is a hallowed place where heaven touches earth and illness and disability cease to have power. The parts of individuals that are broken are not denied or hidden but met with care and love; the aspects of society and environment that work to *keep us* isolated and broken are either restored or surmounted together. The last are first; the ones who need help are helped; the relationships among body, soul, community, and world are smoothed and mended; the spiritual is as real and important as the physical; and suffering of every kind is met with grace upon grace, until it is no longer suffering, but simply one way of *being*.

The grace was delivered by regular, imperfect people, none of whom live in Lourdes. It doesn't *have* to be any other way where you are. It's up to us.

It's very different coming at crises from the other side of brokenness. As Fr. Henri Nouwen wrote in his beautiful meditation *Life of the Beloved*, "The deep truth is that our human suffering need not be an obstacle to the joy and peace we so desire, but can become, instead, the means *to* it."[1] He was writing to a nonreligious friend about the specific and precise ways God calls us to be his beloved: he chooses us, blesses us, breaks us, and gives us to the world. These four movements are echoes of the eucharistic prayer at every Mass: the bread is taken up, blessed, broken, given. On a personal level, though, the movements are each exquisitely and perfectly tailored to the individual. *This is your cross, and I am not going to take it away from you.* Our individual brokenness defines us as much as any blessing God has granted, and it points us toward our ultimate mission: to love.

In our bodies and in our souls, the blessing and the breaking come to us all. They are inevitable, they are communal, and they are outward facing. After his falls, Jesus' greatest defeat was his triumph. Resurrected with his wounds, he picked up his broken apostles, joined them together, dusted them off, and set them about their tasks of building his kingdom. They were transformed both as individuals and as a community. They were given to the world, wounds and all . . . as we and you, too, have been chosen, blessed, broken, given.

Epilogue

An exceedingly high number of the pilgrims who volunteer in Lourdes with the Order of Malta were, in fact, malades or caregivers themselves first. I was introduced to dozens.

The one whose cancer is in remission and who came back to volunteer.

The one whose child has a congenital physical disability and who came back to volunteer.

The one who was paralyzed by a stroke and came back to volunteer—in his wheelchair.

The one whose husband died during the pilgrimage but who still finished the pilgrimage—and continued to return as a volunteer.

The one who experienced an instantaneous cure in the baths, who went in on a gurney and walked out on her own feet, whose case is currently being reviewed by the Lourdes Medical Bureau to be certified as one of the official miracles of the apparition site. She returned as a volunteer.

These pilgrims are united by one thing: a compassion driven by experience. They are uniformly unwilling to be limited by their brokenness; instead, it's a springboard to mercy and love in action. That hopeful defiance in the face of strife—that tested-and-tried belief that God is present even in the most painful and unmanageable circumstances of life—yields fruit and calls forth blessings. The sharing of wounds and the compassionate movement that soothes and anoints those raw places are each a tick forward in God's perpetual engine of mercy. A single step in faith, especially forward through darkness, will be repaid a thousandfold by our loving Father in heaven, who is always, always running out to meet us and multiply our feeble efforts.

Such faith enables us to stand up, dust ourselves off, and go about choosing to do one—just one at a time—of a million possible tiny acts of love. Sometimes the step is the offering of a balm, a word, or a gift; other times it is the receiving. By these acts, the kingdom of God is built on earth. God's mercies are new every morning, and those mercies are made manifest by us: his chosen, blessed, broken people. Our brokenness is his gift to us, a kiss of peace that we are meant to share.

Oscar's brokenness is still our family's greatest gift, a contradictory sign of Christ's peace. As of this writing, he is five years old. He still does not walk or talk. He makes slow and incremental gains toward his goals in speech, occupational, and physical therapy.

He has, more importantly, cultivated a delightful sense of humor. If he is sitting on your lap and you're looking somewhere else, instead of at him, he slowly, slowly leans over until his face is directly in your line of sight, then smiles widely and throws his arms around your neck. He takes deep, abiding pleasure in the noise of his fingers squeaking along the sides of a balloon, and the noise of it popping—better still if it's full of water. He immediately ascertains the location of the nearest water source in every new setting, and he crawls (his primary mode of locomotion) with alarming speed and alacrity straight for it. If he can't find a sink or a toilet, he settles happily for abandoned coffee cups, which are plentiful in this house, easy pickings for a child whose height and curiosity outpace his awareness of safety.

His earthly pilgrimage of joy continues in an ever-expanding social circle. I once wondered aloud whether my boy would ever be capable of surprising me, ever appear in my doorway with a fistful of wildflowers. One month after he began preschool in 2019, Oscar brought home a valentine he had made with his teachers' help, scribbles and dots and hearts forged by his own hand, and I was surprised and delighted beyond measure. Although I had been scared to release him to the care of strangers—just as I'd been scared to release the stroller handle to Carole in the airport terminal in May 2017—his teachers have repeatedly proven the depth of their care for him. When I dropped him off one day, his favorite teacher stopped to remark, "I love the way he raises his little eyebrow at you when he's thinking." I never told her about this, one of my favorite quirks of his—he has his father's Wilkens eyebrow. His teacher seeks out and delights in his quirks and his habits, his stubbornness and his power.

At the time we applied for the Lourdes pilgrimage, Oscar's list of medications and diagnoses and specialists seemed insurmountably complicated. Each list has at least doubled since that time. We still tweak medication and diet. He presents new, challenging, and sometimes unmanageable symptoms nearly every month. We make unexpected visits to the ER that end in unexpected hospital admissions. And our other five children still agree, without any resentment among them, that he is the best of us. Each night they pray in thanksgiving that Oscar is so happy, and in supplication that he will always stay this happy.

As in Lourdes, we attend every Mass with Oscar in his wheeled conveyance, but at home it's a bright orange wheelchair instead of a blue voiture. He still (mostly) sits placidly before the altar, content to be with us and with Jesus. I remember a Sunday recently when the bells rang during the Consecration, and Oscar stiffened. My body immediately went to red alert, but he was stiff with attention, not a seizure. He stared at the host as the priest raised it and then turned a silent, wondering gaze to me. He looked back at the altar, worshipful, then back to me, twice more, a beaming ecstasy overtaking his entire face and body. "Do you see him, Mama? It's *Jesus*," his eyes rang out.

He is our Mary Magdalene, joyfully recognizing the presence of the Lord in our midst, announcing it with his whole being.

Our family has returned to Lourdes every year since Oscar's pilgrimage. In 2018, one of our daughters accompanied me—I as a volunteer, she as a beret-topped page distributing Lourdes water and lively antics. She received her First Communion in the grotto, the same weekend of her brother's first seizure, the same weekend as his bathing and anointing. The first weekend in May carries the significance of a birthday, anniversary, or death in our family. In a way, it is all three: the birth of our hope, the anniversary of our most personal consecration to the Blessed Mother, the death of our old ways of believing and being. In 2019, Todd volunteered, working with a teenager whose challenges are very similar to Oscar's, catching a glimpse of one possible future, a decade down the road. He joined this young malade and his little sister onstage for a rousing rendition of "Take Me Out to the Ballgame" at the pilgrimage talent show.

The plan for 2020 was upended, as so many plans were, by the arrival of the coronavirus. Not only was the Order of Malta pilgrimage canceled, but the Lourdes sanctuary closed its gates to all pilgrims for the first time in its 160 years of existence. During the first weekend of May, from our couch in Texas, we watched Mass offered in the grotto for the intentions of the Order of Malta worldwide, as did the two malades whose applications we had sponsored from their own homes. We were divided in human space, but united in God's time with the people whom we have come to love so dearly as brothers and sisters in Christ.

Some plans cannot be derailed, even by pandemics. I was invested as a Dame of Malta in the fall of 2019, and Todd as a Knight in 2020; we have spent the time before and since in charitable works for the Order of Malta in central Texas. The call to charity has taken on a new urgency amid the bizarre uncertainty of societal lockdown and enigmatic disease. Beneath that quagmire, though, the larger call shapes the rest of our lives: we will return—again and again, spiritually and physically—to the waters of Lourdes, source of healing, community, and maternal love.

Why Lourdes? Why not demonstrate that trust in Austin, or Cincinnati, or wherever it is you happen to live right now?

Pilgrimage allows us to disconnect from our everyday circumstances. It throws us off-balance and strips away our defenses. We are forced to relinquish all the little rituals we use to protect, shield, and hide ourselves from grace in our everyday lives. No Netflix or

Facebook. No whiskey or caramel macchiatos. (Okay, some whiskey.) Going on pilgrimage costs us something.

What it gains us, though, is more than worth the cost, and the thing that is gained is very often not the thing we thought we were looking for in the first place. I thought I was taking Oscar on pilgrimage to be fixed. Instead, what God fixed was my own prideful insistence that brokenness is something to run from, a burden instead of a blessing. What was fixed was my fear that brokenness signaled God's lack of love for us—or worse, God's curse.

What was fixed was my stubborn and idiotic notion that I had to shoulder the cross alone. *I will be with you, and I will help you, but it is yours to carry.*

My eyes were opened to the deep brokenness all around me and inside me, inside everyone, normally so well hidden and tidily packaged away. In stripping away my defenses, burdening me with a weight far too heavy to carry alone, and planting me among the ruins that were the inevitable result, God forced me to accept my need to be served. He reached straight into my brokenness, all the way through to my heart. He used the hands of the people around me, those who had been broken before me, to do his reaching.

Most importantly, God taught me to fully inhabit my own brokenness, to fully celebrate my son's, and to use them both to walk alongside others who are suffering—just as Christ walked the earth with his wounds, empowering his disciples to overcome chaos, subjugation, and persecution with divinely inspired love.

To be with and to help—our task is twofold. We are called to accept accompaniment and to reach forth with our wounded hands.

The light gets in through the cracks. If we weren't broken, we would never acknowledge our need for God's mercy. We live as physical bodies, so this need is made real in physical terms. We need a community to physically manifest, and to truly understand, God's profound love—bodies to call it forth into the world with the work of hands and feet, bodies to accept it with humility and gratitude. That need for each other, that necessary exchange of love, is God's greatest gift to us.

We are all needy. We are all *malades*. Our maladies teach us that we belong to each other, when we yield to the weight of them. Eventually those maladies lead us together—at the end of our beloved, broken, beautiful lives—home again to heaven.

Acknowledgments

Iam grateful to my team at Ave Maria Press, especially to Heidi Hess Saxton, my editor, for bringing our family's story to life in these pages. Any editor who calmly talks authors off manuscript-related ledges only four weeks before a deadline—and throws in a bonus prayer for peace of heart—is a real treasure.

Thank you to Michelle Buckman and Janet Reid, who offered heaven-sent guidance at crucial moments to bring the right book to the right people. And to my crew of beta readers (Kate Rademacher, Cammie Fleming, and Rebecca Ramsay) and blog readers: it would be impossible to repay you for slogging through early, *very* messy versions of this work, but I definitely owe you each a margarita.

The making of this book depended on the support of several communities: our children's schools, teachers, and godfamilies (the Gahans, Heneises, Haunspergers, Politos, Bargers, and Walshes); our parish and priests at St. Louis King of France in Austin, Texas, especially Fr. James Misko; and our beloved nannies, Faith "Abby" Luster and Hayley Brown. Thank you for creating the space where writing—and healing—could happen.

Thank you to our Lourdes podparents and the Order of Malta, who have altered the course of our lives—in particular, Kim Gillespie, Carole Less, Ryan Young, Amy Cattapan, John Sauder, Don Patteson, and Monsignor Frank Caldwell. This book is one small token of our gratitude for the awesome grace you gifted to us. One addendum: Oscar had five podparents, not four as recounted in this book, but one was sick during the entire pilgrimage, aiding us with her prayers and offered-up suffering instead of her hands. Her loving, cloistered service to our family is not forgotten. Thank you, Katherine Baxter.

Thank you to our outstanding medical team at home, who kept Oscar strong enough to make this pilgrimage. Dr. Gabriel Millar; Dr. Karen Keough, Patti, and Amber at CNCA; Dr. Rahel Berhane, Bridget, and the entire CCC team; and our therapists Carole, Chelsea, Katie, Joann, Danyle, and Amberly. We are eternally grateful for the many ways you have cared for and loved our boy—and our whole family.

Thank you to Amy Robertson, who lived every day of these experiences with me from thousands of miles away, answered every hysterical message with compassion and peace, and let me say the dreadful things I couldn't say to anyone else. You walked through the valley of the shadow of death with me, when it wasn't your valley, and I love you for it.

My parents and Todd's have always provided the just-in-time logistical and emotional aid we need to thrive, especially during our most troubled days. Thank you to Sara and Stefan (†) Wilkens and Phil and Sylvia Adessa for all the ways you fill in our gaps, for the extra doses of love and attention our children crave, and for your unfailing support of us as parents and humans. We could never have done (or continue to do) any of this without you. To Jim Adessa and Libby and Brendan Hurley, thank you for your steadfast, unflinching love, in the dark and the light alike.

Thank you to our older children, Ambrose, Benny, Miriam, Stefan, and Theda: I know what these experiences, both the living and the writing of them, have cost you. Your generosity, resilience, and faith through adversity are the lesson in sainthood I didn't know I needed. You kept me at the feet of Jesus when nothing else could, so if I *do* eventually make it to heaven, it will be because your precious souls were my tether. Thank you for your love and your patience with your still-imperfect mother.

To Oscar: thank you, always and forever, for the unvarnished treasure of your presence, your deep smiles, and your easy peace. Thank you for being God's instrument in revealing and restoring what was *malade* in me.

Todd, you have encountered me at my absolute worst and sheltered and loved me there. You are the face, hands, and feet of Christ to me every day, my greatest teacher in servant love. Thank you for choosing me, marrying me, staying with me, and always calling me to be a better person than I was the day before. Thank you for the gift of every single one of our children, and for all the times you tap in when I am tapped out. Thank you for hugs and space and words and silence in proper measure, in an acceptable time. A suitable thank-you for any of that will take a lifetime; I intend to keep trying, and failing, and trying again. I love you. (xoxox)

Thank you, Lord, for this story and my role in it. To God be the glory.

+JMJ+

ECCE, FIAT, MAGNIFICAT

A Discussion Guide on the Healing Power of Surrender and Community

This six-week discussion guide walks through the significant moments in our family's healing journey outlined in *Awakening at Lourdes* and invites you to apply the three movements—acknowledgment, acceptance, and praise—to your own life.

We are all wounded, in body, spirit, or both. We are all in need of God's merciful healing, and we must not flinch from confronting our own vulnerability if we are to continue moving toward heaven (*Ecce*). We need to discern his will for ourselves as individuals, in the context of our communities, and within the heart of our marriages and families (*Fiat*). And finally, we must cultivate an attitude of praise, giving thanks for whatever (and whomever!) the Lord has seen fit to send into our lives (*Magnificat*).

Each week begins with Mary's own words. Though they are few, only a handful of recorded conversations in scripture, they are powerful lessons in each of these three movements. At home, as in Lourdes, Mary is our mother and our first teacher in how to be human—and a saint.

The next section contains a reflection and questions pertaining to sections of the book. After answering, use the final scripture passage to illuminate and deepen your responses. As you step into our story and our transformation, I hope you will find your own story—and your own transformation of the heart—in these words.

Week 1

Ecce

Chapters 1–4: Acknowledge Your Humanity

Ecce ancilla domini.
Behold, I am the handmaid of the Lord.
—Luke 1:38

Before any healing can begin, we must acknowledge that God holds all the cards. He made us, we belong to him, and we trust that he will work out every detail of our lives for his good and his glory.

At least, that's the case in the long run. In the short term, we must continue to live in a fallen world where the existence of disease and disability—both physical and spiritual—is a daily trial. Mary's words in Luke 1:38 remind us of our littleness and that we are all called to subjugate our own wills in favor of the moments God has planned out for us.

While Mary was conceived without sin and resided perfectly within the center of God's will for her, you and I weren't and don't. Even so, we are called to stand before God, exactly as we are, and offer our entire selves. His plan for us, in our brokenness, is as good and as holy as was his plan for Mary, in her sinlessness.

1. What particular brokenness or cross weighs heavily on you? (It may be physical, spiritual, or both.)
2. What might holiness and wholeness look like, with respect to your answer above, *even if* the cross is not removed?
3. What aspects of your life are you resisting turning over to God's control? What hinders you?

4. How would it feel to thank God for the truth that you are fearfully,
    wonderfully made, including (not in spite of) your brokenness?
    Try at least one way of thanking him explicitly, perhaps sharing
    with a friend, writing it down, or offering it in prayer.

Take It to Prayer

Out of the depths I call to you, LORD;
Lord, hear my cry!
May your ears be attentive
to my cry for mercy.

Psalm 130:1–2

Week 2

Fiat (Part 1)

Chapters 5–9: Surrender to God's Will for You

Fiat mihi secundum verbum tuum.
May it be done to me according to your word.
—Luke 1:38

The second half of Mary's response to the angel's message is simply this: surrender. She accepted God's plan as much as Christ did in Gethsemane, when he prayed, "Not my will but yours be done" (Lk 22:42).

Maybe you, like me, frequently get stuck at the "take this cup away" part of Christ's prayer in the garden, or the "How can this be?" question that was Mary's first reply. Worse still, maybe you, like me and like the woman whose medical equipment failed on pilgrimage, cannot open your hands to receive the gifts God is offering, because you're clinging too tightly to what you've already got under your control.

Have the courage, in the questions below, to move beyond doubts and fears and step forward into the mission God sets before you, even when the endgame seems frightening and unclear.

1. What are the benefits and drawbacks of continuing to pray for a specific outcome to a felt need, like the persistent widow before the unjust judge? (See Lk 18:1–8.)
2. What other kinds of prayer does God invite you to try, besides petitionary prayer asking for your desires? How can you incorporate those into your daily life?

3. How can you rest in trust when God clearly answers a prayer, but not in the way you hoped or expected?

4. What concrete steps can you take to surrender one of the burdens in your life? What's an initial, achievable, small surrender? What's an ideal long-term goal that moves you closer to heaven?

Take It to Prayer

In this you rejoice, although now for a little while you may have to suffer through various trials, so that the genuineness of your faith, more precious than gold that is perishable even though tested by fire, may prove to be for praise, glory, and honor at the revelation of Jesus Christ.

1 Peter 1:6–7

Week 3

Fiat (Part 2)

Chapters 10–14: Alive in the Body of Christ

He has helped Israel his servant,
remembering his mercy,
according to his promise to our fathers,
to Abraham and to his descendants forever.

—Luke 1:54–56

In giving us the Church, Christ has given us the gift of himself and of each other. He did not leave us alone. First, he sent us the Holy Spirit to console and strengthen each one of us, from St. Peter right down to you. But with that strength, he invites us to turn toward our brothers and sisters, binding up the brokenhearted with our own wounded hands.

Mary reminds us, in her beautiful prayer of praise, that God has already promised us mercy. We can trust that he does not forget his promises. We too are Abraham's descendants, and the promise is *forever*. That promise is occasionally lived out through miraculous intervention, but more often through God's people.

The Israelites' long sojourn in the desert was a pilgrimage. While every moment of our lives is, in one sense, a pilgrimage toward heaven, we all undergo intense periods when we feel that we are wandering far outside of our everyday plans—sometimes intentionally, sometimes against our will.

To remember our birthright as a pilgrim people means to remember that we journey *together* and that our bondage and our wanderings (both the small ones and the lifelong one) are meant to bring us closer to God, who is our ultimate destination.

1. What aspects of your life can you see, in hindsight, were periods or places where God allowed you to journey through bondage or confusion?

2. How has God already moved in your life, through his community of believers?

3. How can you bring the mindset of pilgrimage into your everyday existence? (For example, a pilgrimage mindset can include the cost of giving up routine comforts, the surrender of control and decisions, the uncertainty of letting God's plan unfold in its own time.)

4. How does your outlook shift if you choose to see your own story of pilgrimage as one small reflection of God's larger story of salvation history? If God could bring the Israelites to the Promised Land, what might he be doing with you?

Take It to Prayer

Happy are those who love you,
and happy are those who rejoice in your peace.
Happy too are all who grieve
over all your afflictions,
For they will rejoice over you
and behold all your joy forever.

—Tobit 13:14

Week 4

Fiat (Part 3)

Chapters 15–18: No Longer Two but One Flesh

Your father and I have been looking for you with great anxiety.
—Luke 2:48

Mary and Joseph endured their own heart-stopping, world-over-turning moment of panic during Jesus' childhood, when he disappeared from their caravan on the way home from Jerusalem. I wish Todd and I had followed this holy couple's example: rather than separating or finger-pointing, they simply banded together, searching anxiously until they made their way together back to Jesus' side.

Wouldn't the world, and every marriage, be better if we could simply acknowledge when we have gone astray, turn toward each other, and run back to Jesus hand in hand?

I know—*I know!*—this is easier said than done. It's natural, even well-intentioned, to want to shield our spouse from the weight of our individual burdens. Goodness knows my husband had enough of his own. And it's well within our fallen human nature to misunderstand and accuse someone whose response to trauma is different than our own.

But marriage is a sacrament, and each sacrament carries its unique graces. We can only access those graces if we fully embrace the particular act of that sacrament. In the case of marriage, this means a very special and intimate kind of vulnerability, choosing to expose our tender underbellies in a thousand daily moments, living as two hearts in one flesh.

1. What have you been hiding from your spouse, trying to carry on your own? Why? What effects do you see from those choices?

2. How has your spouse's response to your own burdens hurt you in the past? What do you need so that you are able to forgive that hurt? Consider a frank discussion, counseling, or even Confession, if you have been harboring resentment.

3. Choose one burden to surrender, then ask directly for your spouse's help with it. Ask Jesus to help you expose this weakness in charity and humility.

4. To what burden of your spouse's have you hardened your heart? Ask the Blessed Mother to help you extend healing instead. Choose (at least) one word of mercy and one example of active love, then offer them.

Take It to Prayer

I, then, a prisoner for the Lord, urge you to live in a manner worthy of the call you have received, with all humility and gentleness, with patience, bearing with one another through love, striving to preserve the unity of the spirit through the bond of peace.

—Ephesians 4:1–3

Week 5

Magnificat (Part 1)

Chapters 19–22: Rejoice Always

Magnificat anima mea Dominum.
My soul proclaims the greatness of the Lord.
—Luke 1:46

God does not reach down to miraculously heal all sickness and all disability, physical or spiritual. In fact, Jesus himself rose from the grave with his scars and his wounds on full display. His resurrection, his glorified body, were not what anyone expected.

Healing does not always look like what we imagined. Oscar did not leave Lourdes in a state of perfect physical health, but he *was* unmistakably changed. My spiritual health and our marriage were restored, but still new, frail, and tender—a work in progress.

How could we help but sing, though, when we compared our homecoming to where we had started? How could we help but be uplifted by the infectious joy of that hallowed place, where suffering is united to Christ's Cross and where we are united to one another? How could we walk away unchanged from the example of our fellow brothers and sisters in Christ singing God's praise, with one voice, amid the worst trials of their lives?

Mary's *Magnificat*, spoken to her cousin after the revelation of her unintended teenage pregnancy, invites us to recall the greatness of the Lord, always and everywhere. There is no dark corner that his love does not reach.

1. Who do you know who has been an example of Christian joy during suffering? It may be someone you know in real life, or perhaps the story of a saint.
2. Where do you hear the whisper of God's movement in your trials so far—or, as a friend once put it, experience the "aftertaste" of his presence?
3. What expectations are you harboring about healing in your life? How does the story of the Resurrection invite you to modify those expectations, or let them go entirely?
4. Try this simple daily exercise: thank God for three good things.

Take It to Prayer

Rejoice always. Pray without ceasing. In all circumstances give thanks, for this is the will of God for you in Christ Jesus.

—1 Thessalonians 5:16–18

Week 6:
Magnificat (Part 2)

Chapters 23–Epilogue:
Go, Therefore, and Make Disciples

Do whatever he tells you.
—John 2:5

T he context of this Marian utterance, we remember, is a wedding that has run out of wine. Disaster! How many times in our own lives have we completely run out of the thing that seems essential?

We can always come to Christ with our desperation, our utter lack of anything necessary for the situation at hand. But the transformative moment happens when we listen and respond. The steward, a lowly member of the staff, honors Mary's directive. The needs at the wedding were fulfilled because Mary insisted that everyone do whatever Christ commanded, however ludicrous, with no conditions—and also *because they did.*

Lourdes was a trash heap that is now a world-renowned pilgrimage site because Bernadette did what was asked of her, even in her weakness and infirmity. Our family was healed because our community, even the suffering ones, honored those holy nudges to serve us, in Lourdes and in Austin—and we were healed even further when we used that experience to direct our own service.

God is calling you, too—even in your neediness—to move out into the world with his mercy. Your blessings and your brokenness are for others.

1. A charism is a gift that God has given you to be used specifically for the building of his kingdom. What are *your* charisms? (For example, one of mine is writing!)

2. Who has God placed in your life that could benefit from those charisms?

3. How can you discern the difference between the moments when you are being called to rest and receive and the moments when you are called to go forth and give?

4. Choose three small acts of mercy, either corporal or spiritual. Now go do them!

Take It to Prayer

The community of believers was of one heart and mind, and no one claimed that any of his possessions was his own, but they had everything in common.

—Acts 4:32

Notes

6. My Faith Is Not Equal to My Situation

1. Richard Gilliard, "The Servant Song" (Chicago: Brentwood Benson, 1977).

2. Gilliard, "The Servant Song."

7. On Holding On and Letting Go

1. Frank Deford, *Alex: The Life of a Child* (New York: Open Road Media: 2015), 63.

8. Prostrate in the Mud

1. C. S. Lewis, *A Grief Observed* (San Francisco: HarperOne, 2015), 6–7.

11. The Dark Night of the Soul

1. John of the Cross, *Dark Night of the Soul* (Mineola, NY: Dover, 2003), 25.

18. In the Footsteps of Bernadette

1. Shauna Niequist, *Bread and Wine: A Love Letter to Life around the Table with Recipes* (Grand Rapids, MI: Zondervan, 2013), 250.

20. Life Wins

1. Teresa of Calcutta, quoted in Michael E. Gaitley, *33 Days to Morning Glory: A Do-It-Yourself Retreat in Preparation for Marian Consecration* (Stockbridge, MA: Marian Press, 2011), 75–76.

2. Michael E. Gaitley, *33 Days to Morning Glory: A Do-It-Yourself Retreat in Preparation for Marian Consecration* (Stockbridge, MA: Marian Press, 2011), 76.

24. Rise, Take Up Your Mat

1. C. S. Lewis, *The Problem of Pain* (San Francisco: HarperOne, 2015), 101.

25. Chosen, Blessed, Broken, Given

1. Henri Nouwen, *Life of the Beloved: Spiritual Living in a Secular World* (New York: Crossroad, 2002), 95.

Christy Wilkens is a writer for *CatholicMom.com*, *Blessed Is She*, and *Accepting the Gift*. She is a Dame of Magistral Grace in the Sovereign Military Order of Malta, which she joined after a pilgrimage to Lourdes with her husband, Todd, and their youngest son, Oscar—a trip that was sponsored by the organization.

Wilkens is a lector and catechist at her parish. She has appeared on *The Jennifer Fulwiler Show* on SiriusXM and has been featured in the Order of Malta American Association newsletter, *Hospitallers*. Wilkens earned a bachelor's degree from Rice University and a master's degree from the University of North Carolina at Chapel Hill. She is pursuing a bachelor's degree in nursing.

The Wilkenses live with their six children in the Austin, Texas, area.

Christywilkens.com
Facebook: @faithfulnotsuccessful
Twitter: @csawilkens
Instagram: @csawilkens
Pinterest: @csawilkens

Jennifer Fulwiler is a comedienne, podcaster, and author of several books, including *Something Other than God*.

AVE MARIA PRESS

Founded in 1865, Ave Maria Press,
a ministry of the Congregation of
Holy Cross, is a Catholic publishing
company that serves the spiritual and
formative needs of the Church and its
schools, institutions, and ministers;
Christian individuals and families; and
others seeking spiritual nourishment.

———◈———

For a complete listing of titles from

Ave Maria Press

Sorin Books

Forest of Peace

Christian Classics

visit www.avemariapress.com

AVE MARIA PRESS
Notre Dame, IN
A Ministry of the United States Province of Holy Cross